T0148386

The Winter's Journey of My Youth
A Memoir

Also by Helen Studley

Life of a Restaurant
The Chicken for Every Occasion Cookbook

The Winter's Journey of My Youth
A Memoir

Helen Studley

iUniverse, Inc.
New York   Bloomington

The Winter's Journey of My Youth
A Memoir

iUniverse books may be ordered through booksellers or by contacting:

iUniverse
1663 Liberty Drive
Bloomington, IN 47403
www.iuniverse.com
1-800-Authors (1-800-288-4677)

Because of the dynamic nature of the Internet, any Web addresses or links contained in this book may have changed since publication and may no longer be valid. The views expressed in this work are solely those of the author and do not necessarily reflect the views of the publisher, and the publisher hereby disclaims any responsibility for them.

ISBN: 978-1-4401-4019-8 (sc)
ISBN: 978-1-4401-4021-1 (hc)
ISBN: 978-1-4401-4020-4 (ebook)

Printed in the United States of America

iUniverse rev. date: 6/18/2009

To my grandson Luke

Table of Contents

HAMBURG

Acknowledgment

The book would not have happened without the enthusiastic support, sensitive prodding, and thoughtful editing of my friend Erica Marcus.

Preface

Do we need another Holocaust memoir, and should I write one?

No, I didn't want to write one; at least not the part about the concentration camps. That was a past I did not wish to revisit. My real life started when I came to New York in May 1946. It was a good life, full of love and fulfilled ambition.

One of the ambitions was to be involved in music; the other was to be a writer. I combined the two by writing liner notes, opera synopses, and bios of performing artists for several record companies. I also wanted to travel and eventually opened my own travel agency. That led to writing travel newsletters and travel articles for major magazines. When my husband and I opened a restaurant, I wrote our newsletter, published two cookbooks, and established myself as a food and wine writer.

Besides, I had already written a war memoir forty years ago. I had called it *Züge* (Trains) because so many events in my youth were connected to trains. I never did anything with the manuscript; I put it into a box and stashed it into the back of a closet. Following the success of my second cookbook, my literary agent suggested I write my memoir. I wrote a five-chapter proposal and called it "Hiding in Berlin." The market, however, was saturated with Holocaust stories. *Züge* went back into the closet.

In July 2008, my sister Ruth died. Ruth, who was childless, had been the last link to my past; it was a double loss. Shortly thereafter, one my nephews asked me about my life in Germany. He was apologetic about not having brought it up before: "I didn't want to bother you." It seemed a forbidden subject; nobody else had ever asked. I thought of Luke, my five-year old grandson. By the time he'll be old enough to ask, I will most likely be dead. I had a story to tell, and that story acquired an urgency that made me put all other writing projects on the back burner.

I filled out the proposal for "Hiding in Berlin" with five additional chapters. Before sending the manuscript to the publisher, I wanted my friend Erica Marcus to read it. Erica had been the editor for my book *Life of a Restaurant,* an account of the years during which my husband and I owned *La Colombe d'Or* restaurant. Erica agreed to help "polish" the work. She liked my style and the various vignettes but felt one important element was missing: I never talked about the camps and for good reason. I never intended to write about them; reliving those experiences would cost me too much pain. Besides, I believed that including the camp experiences would sound like bragging: "look what I went through." On top of it I wondered: "does anybody really care?"

Erica understood, but she begged me to reconsider. She didn't have to spell it out, but it became clear: to avoid having to confront the past I had produced "Holocaust Lite." I went back to the *Züge* manuscript and was shocked. What I had written ten years after the war was raw stuff, still fresh in my mind. In the meantime, I had forgotten many specific incidents of horrors and humiliations.

I wrote my first camp flashback, and it disrupted my present, everyday life—the past invaded the present. I suffered all kinds of pain and was convinced I had cancer. Reluctantly I went to see my doctor. He gave me a clean bill of health. To reestablish my usual optimistic outlook, I decided to forget about the memoir for the time being and wrote some proposals to the various magazines I regularly write for. But whatever topic I considered seemed trivial compared to what I had experienced during the war. Whether or not I wanted to, the memoir had become my priority. I realized I would have to finish the book in spite of the trauma it would entail. Part of that decision may have been born out of my vanity as a writer. I wanted the book to be as good as possible. Then there was Luke. At the end, I wrote the book for myself.

I choose Schubert's "Die Winterreise" (The Winter's Journey) as the title because the song cycle deals with love, loss, and longing—sentiments that echoed mine during those difficult years of the war. Schubert continued to be my companion as I traveled back in time.

Helen Studley
New York
2008

A Swim Before the Storm

Summer 1938

June 15, 1938—Opening day of our local swimming club. I could hardly wait to show off my bathing suit, sporting the insignia I had received at the end of last year's season for having passed the forty-five minute swimming endurance challenge.

If it hadn't been for Father (I called him Väti), I would have failed the test, because it required a dive from the three-meter board. I had often jumped from the one-meter board and didn't think that two more meters would be that different. But, when I stood at the edge of the high diving board and looked down, I got so scared I felt it in the pit in my stomach.

I had turned, ready to give up, when Father appeared on top of the ladder: "Hildegard Less," said Father, addressing me by my full name, "either you jump, or I'll push you. What is it going to be?"

So I jumped. When I emerged from the water, everybody cheered wildly. At nine, I was the youngest member to have earned the award. At the ceremony, Mr. Schlösser, the club director, congratulated me and told Father I was a spunky girl. The director also said Father was a pillar of our community and thanked him, as head of the local chamber of commerce, for having been instrumental for the merchants' generous contribution toward the construction of the Olympic-size pool.

Bicycling to the club a year later, I fantasized about my welcoming reception. But when I reached the gate, I saw a sign: "Jews not welcome."

I nearly went past it. Jews? What did that have to do with me? And then I realized: everything. In fact, the sign might as well say that I, my sister Ruth, and Father were not welcome since we were the only Jews in town.

I stood there, stunned. I hopped back on my bike and nearly landed in a ditch because my hands were shaking. Still, I got back to our house in record time, lucky to find Father in his office at the back of the store.

"Unbelievable," he said. "Those good-for-nothing upstarts who call themselves Nazis. A few years ago, they didn't have a pot to piss in, and now they talk about ruling the world. Don't take it to heart. Mark my word, they won't last."

A few days later my sister Ruth received a note from an organization inviting us to use the old bathing facility on the river Biese, which they had taken over after everyone else had abandoned it once the pool had been built. Ruth went to inquire.

"They are very nice," she reported, "shocked about what happened at the club."

"Who are these people," asked Father. "Do we know them?"

"No, we don't," said Ruth. "They belong to a special sect."

"A special sect?" Father was skeptical.

Ruth hesitated. Then she blushed. "They are nudists."

"Nudists?" cried Father. "Forget it. It's not for us."

"I know it's not for you," said Ruth, "but I don't mind. They are cultured people, and they won't expect us to strip. If you don't mind, I'd like to go."

The following afternoon, as Ruth got her swimming gear together, she turned to me. "Are you coming along?"

It was one of those grown-up questions I hated because there was no escape. Like Father asking me if I minded carrying his rifle while he was on his way to the hunting club. Didn't he know I was afraid of guns? And nudists? The very idea of meeting them made me squirm. But, that was just it—never in all my life would I turn Father or Ruth down. Father was my idol. He was one of the most respected persons in Osterburg: owner of a big shoe store, member of the chamber of commerce, the hunting club, and the weekly *Skat* game. In addition he was a volunteer fireman.

Every day, after the midday meal, he took me along on his walk. I was proud to be seen in his company, as he doffed his hat to neighbors, chatted with colleagues, stopped at the cigar store, the pharmacy, or at the hat maker. He talked to me like a grown-up: about Copernicus and his stars, Amundsen and the South Pole, the importance of telephone wires, alligators, the Sahara desert, and his favorite topic—World War I and how he had earned his medal.

Ruth was fifteen years my senior. Two years before, when Mutti had died, Ruth returned home to run our household and take care of me. She did a much better job than Mother, who had suffered from migraines and nine out of ten times couldn't be disturbed.

Ruth was the opposite. She had studied childhood education, which she now practiced on me. She built a puppet theater, made the puppets, and acted as puppeteer. She taught me how to knit clothes for my dolls and encouraged me to write poetry. She knew a million songs, played the guitar, and, at bedtime, read chapters of *Dr. Dolittle*, specially ordered from a shop in Berlin. She had been to Sweden, Hungary, and Switzerland and corresponded with friends she had met there. Best of all, Ruth convinced Father to give in to my pleading about taking piano lessons. I loved the piano and had taught myself to read music. Thanks to Ruth, Father hired Miss Schneider to give me lessons once a week on my family's upright.

The river was walking distance from our house. "Did one

curtsy in front of nudists?" I wondered. "Would there be other children?" I had never seen a naked person before. When we reached the river, our hosts came to greet us. They were stark naked, all of them. The women had hanging breasts; their skin was wrinkled. Most had thinning gray hair. The men looked so weird, I averted my eyes. When they addressed me, I stammered and kept my eyes glued to my sandals. I bolted into the Biese and remained there till it was time to go home.

Ruth convinced me to go back the next day.

"They are kind, don't you think?" she said. "It would be rude not to accept their hospitality."

"Who are they?" I wondered. Without clothes it was hard to tell. Ruth did find out that among the nudists were two former school teachers, a minister, a seamstress, and a piano tuner. They talked about the importance of sunshine, fresh air, and leading a healthy life. They ate raw celery and carrots and something called Knäckebrot, a flatbread that was as hard as a brick.

"Excellent for the digestion," they said, "particularly if eaten with thick yogurt."

They told us that people in Bulgaria lived to be a hundred years old because they ate yogurt every day. Just in case we wanted to live that long, they explained to Ruth how to make this yogurt. Ruth and Minna, our house keeper, made a few batches and served their best effort one evening alongside the Westphalian ham, cervelat, smoked tongue, and liverwurst we usually had for supper.

"What do we have here?" asked Father. To oblige Ruth, he agreed to give it try. After one spoonful, he declared it food fit only for nursing mothers and banned it from the table.

"Don't mention this to our swimming hosts," said Ruth, as if I would do such a thing.

I would have preferred the nudists not to be quite so naked, but I had to admit that they were nice. The women spoiled me and brought presents that once had belonged to their children. They gathered flowers and made a wreath for me to wear. The men left wood carvings especially for me. They seemed as shy as I was in their presence. Once, we were caught in a thunderstorm. Everybody took shelter in the little shack. The nudists quickly wrapped towels around their bodies. "In deference to us," said Ruth later.

Except for Sunday, we went every afternoon. I had forgotten how pleasant it was to swim in the river. Branches of weeping willows dipped into the water; the meadows were full of anemones; occasionally, a cow strayed to the water's edges. From the water I could see windmills, the spires of St. Nikolai Church. and the storks perched at their chimney nests. There was a bridge, known as the mother-in-law bridge. This mother-in-law was ten times worse than Snow White's stepmother. According to rumor, she was so mean to her son's bride that the poor girl had jumped off the bridge, and her body was later found drifting toward the Elbe.

I imagined swimming down the Biese to where it went into the Elbe. The Elbe, I knew from my geography class, was a mighty river that went all the way down to Hamburg, Germany's great harbor from which freighters and ocean liners departed every day.

My only worry was meeting one of my classmates here and having to explain with whom I went swimming. And then, of all people, Ursula Mäder, the biggest loudmouth in my class, appeared one afternoon.

"Swimming in the Biese?" She was dumbfounded. "Why?"

"Just because," I blushed.

Ursula shrugged her shoulders.

The minute she left, I could have kicked myself. Dumb! "Haven't you heard?" I should have said, "I'm training for the Olympics."

Broken Glass

November 1938

I ignored Father's rule not to barge into his office. My news couldn't wait: I was going to be the narrator in this year's Christmas play, performed by the pupils of the Miss Büttner's School for Young Girls. "And it came to pass that a census was taken throughout the land of Jordan"

I knew the part by heart, having heard it last year when I had been one of the three kings and the year before, when I had been a shepherd. This was the first time that one of her fourth graders was to play the narrator my homeroom teacher Fraulein Honing had said, adding that she knew I wouldn't fumble my lines.

"That's my girl, Trulli," Father would say calling me by my nickname. I knew he would be proud.

But instead of Father I found my sister Ruth.

"Where is Väti?"

"At the police station. Sergeant Schmidt came to get him."

"Why? What happened?"

Ruth bit her lower lip. "Actually Schmidt came to arrest Väti."

"Arrest him? You are joking."

Ruth shook her head. "No, I am not. I think it has something to do with us being Jewish. Apparently a Jewish person killed

7

an SS man in Paris, and now the Nazis are taking it out on all Jews."

"Are they crazy?" I didn't understand. "What does Väti have to do with this?"

Nobody cared whether Father was Jewish or not. Why didn't Ruth tell Schmidt there was some mistake? After all, Ruth was a grownup in charge of our household. Schmidt, surely, would listen. He revered Father, who outfitted Schmidt's children with free slippers from our store every Christmas.

There was some good news. My sister Lieselotte had phoned. She was on her way from Berlin to be with us. I was completely taken with Lieselotte, a student of fashion design. In Berlin, she smoked cigarettes and wore high-heeled shoes and silk stockings as fine as spun gold. She polished her fingernails and painted her lips red. Father insisted she take it off before she came to visit because it would shock the provincial Osterburgers.

I went upstairs to our apartment and turned on the radio. Goebbels was screaming. "The Jews will pay for this. Never again will they dare to touch as much as one hair of one of us."

The speech ended with the Horst Wessel song. Afterwards they played the "Donkey Serenade," the latest hit song from an American movie. I went into the kitchen to ask Minna, our housekeeper, what was for supper. But Minna was not around. I began to practice piano and was half way through Debussy's "Golliwogg's Cake Walk" when Ruth appeared. She pulled up a chair.

"The police called: they are keeping Väti overnight. They have orders to take him to another town early tomorrow morning. They said we could come and say good-bye."

Ruth shook her head. "I don't know what they are planning. I told Fraulein Schroeder, Liesle, and Fritz to go home. Come downstairs with me. I'm closing the store."

I loved our store. On Sundays, I would spend hours pulling out boxes, looking at shoes, and making believe I was Fraulein Schroeder, the senior sales lady.

Ruth put out the lights, except the ones in the windows. Father took great pride in his window displays. For the holidays, he hired a professional window dresser from nearby Stendal, the capital of the Altmark.

Lieselotte arrived.

"You can't imagine what's going on in Berlin," she said. "They are rounding up all Jewish men. Nobody knows where they are taking them."

That wasn't all. The Nazis were burning synagogues and had smashed the windows of Jewish store owners. Looking at me, Lieselotte smiled.

"Don't worry," she said. "They won't do that to us. They have too much respect for Väti."

Ruth and Lieselotte went back downstairs. They still had to unpack a shipment of slippers and put the money into the safe.

Ruth turned to me.

"We have to eat something warm," she said. "Minna had planned cauliflower with Hollandaise. Forget the Hollandaise. Just cook the cauliflower. It's easy."

I was dumbfounded. First of all, I had never cooked anything before, and then, didn't Ruth realize that I wasn't allowed near the stove? "Too dangerous for children," according to Minna.

Sensing my hesitation, Ruth gave me an encouraging pat. "I know you can do it."

I lit five kitchen matches just for practice. The real test came with lighting the gas, because the gas turned on the pilot light, which came on like an explosion. My heart was beating so hard, I thought it would jump out of my throat. But how could I disappoint Ruth? Surely, this was a test of my fortitude. What about the water though? Should I fill the kettle and put it on the stove before lighting it, or after? Ruth had neglected to tell me. I decided to get it over with as quickly as possible. I filled the kettle with water and put it on the stove. I said a quick prayer and lit the burner. Then I sat next to the stove and watched the water boil. When I plunged the cauliflower into the water, half of the water spilled out, almost extinguishing the flame. I was getting angry.

Why couldn't we eat the cauliflower raw? Raw vegetables tasted much better than cooked ones. But according to Minna, eating anything raw was barbaric and out of the question. Why not have sandwiches? I envisioned cervelat on rye bread spread with butter and a dill pickle on the side. Better yet, tartar steak. Minna prepared it with goose fat and coarse salt.

The odor of cooked cauliflower snapped me back. What a stench! Pungent like dirty socks. I had no idea whether the cauliflower was cooked or not. My problem was getting it out of the water and transferring it onto the plate. With the help of two large spoons, I managed to lift the cauliflower out of the water and almost had it on the plate when it slid off and landed on the floor. I was tempted to kick it. Instead, I scooped the cauliflower up, put it on the plate, and called my sisters.

And then, after all my efforts, they were not in the mood to eat. Ruth praised me for the cauliflower, but hardly touched it. Neither did Lieselotte. I couldn't bear to look at the thing and had a glass of milk.

When it was time for bed, Ruth came and sat with me. Knowing how scared I was of the dark without Father in the next room, she allowed me leave the light on. The church bell struck. First the four, middle-pitched sounds announcing the hour was about to be chimed. Then came the deep and somber intoning of the mighty bells. One, two, three, four, five, six, seven, eight, nine. It was late.

Once I had been up on the belfry with my class. We walked along the ramparts, high above town, encouraged to enjoy the sweeping view over meadows and fields. Twice a year, on Easter and Christmas morning, a brass band played chorales from the ramparts. I could hear them now: "Ein feste Burg ist unser Gott."

I woke up. I could not make out the sound. Glass? Glass breaking downstairs? It sounded like New Year's Eve, with

10

everybody breaking glass for good luck. But how much of it and why? Was the entire village breaking glass in front of our house?

I ran into the living room, where I met up with my sisters.

"My God," cried Ruth. "They are smashing our store windows."

"Police," I cried. "Call the police."

Ruth shook her head. "Nobody will come. Look, not a single neighbor has put on a light or looked out of the window."

We huddled together, afraid of what might happen next. Would they come after us with clubs? Since we had no synagogue, would they set our house on fire?

When we heard the noise of departing motorcycles, we went downstairs. The store was in shambles; everything was overturned and smashed to pieces. The broken glass was ankle deep.

"Watch out. Don't cut yourself," cried Ruth. "For God's sake, you're barefoot. Go upstairs and put on shoes. Lieselotte and I will clean up."

It was still dark when the three of us set out for the police station. The street lamps swayed back and forth, throwing eerie shadows against the buildings.

"Not a word about last night," Ruth warned. "If Väti asks, tell him everything is fine."

"And don't cry," said Lieselotte. "Remember Väti likes us to be strong."

I wanted none of this.

"Please," I wanted to say, "I am just a child. I don't want to be here. I'm afraid of the police station; it scares me to see Father in such a place."

The police station consisted of a single room, dimly lit. Heubling, the chief of police, stood by the stove, warming his hands. Father sat at the table drinking coffee, served by policeman Schmidt. Father got up slowly. I ran into his arms. He kissed me on the forehead. Then, he held me straight and motioned my sisters to stand next to us.

"Here we are," he said in a loud and clear voice. "We are

honest, law-abiding people and will not suffer shame and humiliation. I do not know what will happen to my daughters when I am gone."

Father fixed his eyes on chief of police Heubling. "Karl," he said, "you and I go back a long time. I ask you as an old friend and fellow officer of our sharpshooter's club do me the honor and shoot us."

"No," I screamed. "Don't."

I darted from Father's grip and fled to the other side of the room. I closed my eyes and covered my ears, waiting for the shot. There was no question in my mind that father's command would be obeyed. But nothing happened. Father came over and removed my hands.

"Here, here" he said. "It's all right. I got carried away. I didn't mean to frighten you."

He struck a cheerful note.

"Come, sit next to me." He took my hand. "Tell me, what did you do last evening?"

I was so relieved to be alive, I gushed.

"You'll never guess."

"You beat your sisters at cards."

"No," I laughed. I looked around the room, hoping that chief of police Heubling and policeman Schmidt would hear.

"I cooked cauliflower for supper."

"You don't say," said Father. "How was it?"

"Awful," I said. "I hated the smell."

"I never cared much for it either," said father. He chuckled.

Looking at his pocket watch, chief of police Heubling cleared his throat: "Moritz, it's time to go. The train leaves at six thirty sharp."

"Schmidt," he said, turning to the policeman, "take Mr. Less's bag and meet us at the station."

Father put on his overcoat, gloves, and the cap he had bought on a recent trip to Scotland. He kissed us. "My three graces," he said. "Don't worry. I will be back soon."

He turned to Heubling: "Whenever you are ready, chief." Father had switched from the familiar address to the formal one. For a moment I thought the two would salute each other, the way they used to when signaling the sharpshooters' summer festivities to begin.

I felt Lieselotte's arm on my shoulder.

"Here, put on your mittens," said Ruth. "It's cold outside."

The three of us went home.

Our Move to Berlin
March 1939

Father had returned home a week after his arrest. He said he had been in a place called Buchenwald but never mentioned details, at least not in my presence. I didn't want to know anyway and never asked any questions. Father had to give up our house and the store. Ruth had obtained a position as a maid in London, a temporary step, she explained, to get out of Germany. Aunt Emma came to Osterburg to help organize our move. Aunt Emma was Mother's youngest sister. She was unmarried. My uncles referred to her as the spinster. I didn't think spinsters had to be pitied. After all, Aunt Emma had her own apartment in Berlin and did pretty much as she pleased. In March 1939, Father and I left Osterburg and moved to Berlin.

Once in Berlin, we moved temporarily into Uncle Sigie's and Aunt Paula's apartment. Uncle Sigie was Father's younger brother. He had a beautiful voice and had wanted to be an opera singer. But his parents did not approve. When Uncle Sigie married Aunt Paula, he joined her father's business. While we stayed with them, I shared a room with their little boy Herbie.

Berlin was to be an interim stop for us until father could get visas to Chile, following Uncle Magnus and Aunt Trude. We would have preferred to go to America like Lieselotte, but Father said our chances were slim. America had a very limited quota for Jews, and the only reason Lieselotte had been so lucky was because she had married Fred, who had applied for an American visa years ago.

A few months after we moved to Berlin, Hitler marched into Poland, a move that prompted England and France to declare war on Germany. Everything was up in the air, and since we might be stranded in Berlin, we moved to Mrs. Jarz's pension on Viktoria-Luise Platz, one of Berlin's most fashionable neighborhoods. Lieselotte, who had lived there for three years before her marriage, had suggested it to Father.

The pension consisted of a nine-room apartment. Father and I had two separate rooms. Mrs. Jarz's quarters looked unlike anything I had ever seen. Figures of cherubs clung to ornate moldings; shawls, fans, mirrors, and pictures covered the walls; figurines of shepherds and young maidens rested on pedestals. There even was a bronze statute of William Tell, his arrow aimed at the apple sitting on top of his son's little head.

Mrs. Jarz and her husband had been ballroom dancers. A picture on her baby grand showed them in a dance pose. Mr. Jarz was smartly dressed in a white tuxedo and white top hat. Mrs. Jarz wore a white tunic with long fringes. Her forehead was covered by a pearl band which sprouted a big feather.

Eight years ago, her husband had died of tuberculosis. No one from Mrs. Jarz's family had come to the funeral.

"They couldn't forgive me for having run off with a dancer and a gentile at that," she said. In the end, Mrs. Jarz's mother had softened and had left the apartment to her.

I was completely taken with Mrs. Jarz. Staying with her had taken a load off my mind. First, Ruth had left and gone to England, and then Lieselotte had left for America. The last thing she said to me as she and Fred boarded the train on the Anhalter Station, was: "Take care of Väti. You are all he has left now."

"I'm too young for that," I wanted to say. "I need somebody to take care of me." And Mrs. Jarz did just that. She took us under her wing as if we were family. She introduced us to her relatives and friends. A frugal cook, she knew how to make the most of the rationed food, took me along marketing, and let me help in the kitchen. In the evening, she played gin rummy with Father and listened to his stories of how he had been a hero in the First World War. She even persuaded Father to give in to my pleading to cut off my braids, which made me look like a hick.

Mrs. Jarz was plump: "full-figured," she called it. From the way Father looked at her, I could tell he approved. Sunday mornings she wore a kimono, a present from Mr. Yoshoka, one of her boarders. Mr. Yoshoka was Japanese, and the consul from Manchuria. Mr. Yoshoka kept a room at the pension, although his stay was always brief. When he returned, it was always a celebration. He brought caviar, foie gras, smoked sturgeon, French cheeses, Belgian chocolate, and real coffee. He gave all of these items to Mrs. Jarz who served them on Sunday for breakfast. After breakfast, Mrs. Jarz smoked a Turkish cigarette, and Father lit a cigar. Mr. Yoshoka did not smoke. Leaning back in the chair, he smiled and nodded approval. Short and chubby, with pudgy feet and slanted eyes, he looked like the statue of Buddha he kept in his room.

Jewish and Other
Degenerate Composers
Summer 1939

I loved Berlin: its wide boulevards, trolley cars, buses, and taxis; the way people dressed and spoke; elevators in the buildings, cafés, and department stores. Berlin had a zoo, museums, theaters, concert halls, and three opera houses. Of course, as Jews we were barred from all of them. But, then, Berlin had a concert hall and an orchestra just for Jews. From conductor to page turner, every member of that orchestra was Jewish.

German composers like Bach, Beethoven, Mozart, Haydn, or Brahms were forbidden. Instead the Jewish orchestra could play music by Jewish and by other degenerate composers. We learned all this from Mr. Friedrich, a flutist, who was a neighbor.

Some degenerate composers, Mr. Friedrich explained, did not conform to Nazi ideology, like those whose art was termed *Kulturbolschevism*. Others were enemies of the Third Reich. Some enemies of the Third Reich had no composers to speak of, like the English or the Norwegians. On the other hand, Russia had so many enemies of the Third Reich composers that the Jewish orchestra could barely keep up with them.

Occasionally, according to Mr. Friedrich, there was some confusion, like Schumann songs with text by Heinrich Heine. Heine was Jewish; Schumann was 100 percent German. The

German lieder singers didn't know what to do; nor did the Jewish ones. It was up to the cultural minister to decide. Schumann usually won, with certain restrictions.

"Reminds me of my situation," said Mrs. Jarz, who was Jewish like us and a widow like Father. But, since Mrs. Jarz's husband had been a gentile, she enjoyed certain privileges.

"There will be a concert next Sunday," said Mr. Friedrich. "If you like, I could get tickets for you."

The concert hall was at the Kommandenten Strasse, in the northern section of Berlin. We took the subway to Alexander Platz from where it was a brief walk. Father had invited Mrs. Jarz to join us. Mrs. Jarz looked stunning in a dark green suit and high heels. Even Father noticed.

The concert hall was packed. People seemed to know each other; they exchanged greetings and waved across the aisles. Sitting between Father and Mrs. Jarz, I felt so happy being here, I barely cared about the concert. The musicians tuned their instruments. I noticed Mr. Friedrich among the players, but was too embarrassed to wave.

Father, who had bought a program, read the selections. The first part consisted of music by degenerate composers.

"Tchaikovsky," he groaned. Father was a Verdi man. *Aida* was his favorite opera. But with Verdi being Italian, who were allies of the Germans, Father was out of luck. When the orchestra played Tchaikovsky's *1812 Overture*, however, Father got into the act. "Boom, boom, broom," he hummed as the bass and kettle drums crashed and banged, imitating canons.

"Eighteen twelve, that's when the Russians beat Napoleon, who had to retreat from Russia," he explained to Mrs. Jarz. "It's a fact. Nobody has ever conquered Russia. It's too vast a country."

Mrs. Jarz agreed. I could tell she admired Father for his knowledge about such things.

The second part of the concert consisted of music by Jewish composers, starting with songs by Gustav Mahler.

"Mahler?" Father shrugged his shoulders. "Never heard of him. Let's see what he can do."

And then the orchestra played Mendelssohn—his Scottish Symphony. Mendelssohn? Mendelssohn was Jewish? I couldn't believe it. I had played his "Children's Pieces" and the "Venetian Boat Song" from "Songs without Words." I loved Mendelssohn! He was a great composer, like a Schumann or a Schubert, and he was one of us?

I hated being Jewish. Being Jewish had robbed me of all the things I liked. Being Jewish frightened me and was no fun. But here was Felix Mendelssohn Bartholdy. What a discovery! If Mendelssohn was Jewish, I didn't mind being Jewish myself.

After the end of the symphony, the audience went wild. They continued to applaud. Nobody left. "Bravo, bravo," they shouted, "*bis, bis*, more." The musicians stayed in their seats. After the fourth curtain call, the conductor bowed briefly to the audience, nodded to the players, and took up his baton.

The "Wedding March" from "Midsummer Night's Dream." I thought I was dreaming. The "Wedding March"? Lieselotte and Fred had walked down the aisle to the tune of the Wedding March. Every single couple I knew or had heard about had done the same. A wedding without the "Wedding March" was unthinkable, and the one who made it possible was Mendelssohn.

Now what would happen to all these German couples? I smiled. No wonder Hitler wasn't married. All this talk about how his heart belonged to the German people. What a joke! Hitler didn't and couldn't ever get married because of our Mendelssohn.

Mrs. Jarz's Pension
Fall 1939

I knew we had to get out of Germany, but why to Shanghai? Shanghai would never have come up if Aunt Hedwig hadn't killed herself. The note to her husband, my Uncle Albert, said she did not want to be a burden to him in a strange land. I knew better. Aunt Hedwig was afraid to travel across Siberia.

"Absolutely safe," Uncle Albert assured Father. "They seal the cars."

Sure they did. Siberia. That's where the Russians sent their criminals. It was so cold in Siberia, people froze to death or were eaten by wolves. We would never reach Shanghai. Uncle Albert seemed unconcerned. He tried to persuade Father that we should join him now since Aunt Hedwig was gone. After all, he said, Father was his favorite brother. We would be a happy family.

I didn't trust Uncle Albert. Three years ago, he had promised me ice skates—I was still waiting. Besides, I thought Father and I were going to Chile. Two containers with most of our belongings had gone to Genoa to be shipped to Santiago.

"There's been a delay with our visas," he said. "Shanghai may be our only alternative. Aunt Hedwig's visa has been paid for and would be transferred over to you. Uncle Albert is sure he can secure a visa for me."

As it turned out, he could not, and that was fine with me.

I spent most of my time helping Mrs. Jarz with household chores. In the mornings, we brought breakfast to the boarders. The first one was for Mr. Ullstein who occupied the large corner room. Mr. Ullstein had been a publisher before the Nazis had closed his family business. His room was so filled with books I thought he had taken half the company's library with him. He wore a hair net, and his teeth were black from chewing charcoal. On days when his horoscope was unfavorable, he stayed in bed.

Mr. Ullstein was married to a woman who was not only pure German but enjoyed special privileges because her sister was married to a high-ranking Nazi official. Although Mr. and Mrs. Ullstein were separated, she also took a room in the pension to afford him a measure of protection.

"I happen to know things that would ruin their careers," she said. "One wrong move toward him," she pointed toward Mr. Ullstein, whom she always addressed in the third person, "and I'll expose them. They are at my mercy."

To be at her mercy, I imagined, was no laughing matter. She was tall and very thin; her skin was as transparent as parchment.

Father said she looked like death warmed over. Warmed over or not, I was in awe of Mrs. Ullstein. She had been to every opera house in Europe and knew Furtwängler and Gieseking first hand. But most important, she put her large record collection at my disposal. I borrowed her records whenever I wanted and played them on Mrs. Jarz's gramophone. Beethoven, Mozart, Schubert, and Schumann were among my favorites.

The boarder in the maid's room was so shy we hardly knew he was there. He never let us come into his room and always took the breakfast tray from me at the door.

"Thank you. Kiss your hand," he said. He had an accent.

"Mr. Brodsky was a well-known actor in Prague," said Mrs. Jarz. "Now he is stateless and penniless." Feeling sorry for him, she frequently treated him to double portions of strawberry jam.

Food was scarce; everyone received food coupons. Ours looked as if they had the measles because they had a J for Jew stamped all over. Jews received no coupons for milk or white bread and could only shop between four and five o'clock in the afternoon, when most of the supplies were gone. None of this fazed Mrs. Jarz, who flattered the sales women in the dairy store, cajoled the green grocer to give her extra portions of kale or turnips, and flirted with the butcher who saved lungs, brain, spleen, and testicles for her. Mrs. Jarz transformed these unsightly organs into soup, headcheese, and sweet-and-sour stew which she served for dinner, which was attended by every boarder ever since an eight o'clock curfew went into effect.

Mrs. Jarz was a very good cook. No one appreciated that more than Father.

"Erna, you have outdone yourself with this stew. What is it?"

"Rabbit," said Mrs. Jarz.

"How do you know it isn't cat?" said Mr. Ullstein.

Everyone laughed. I wondered. After all, Jews had to turn their pets over to the police. What happened to all those Jewish cats and dogs?

As soon as Mrs. Jarz and I had cleared the table and washed the dishes, we would gather in Mr. Ullstein's room for nightly readings of classic plays. Mrs. Ullstein, who assigned the parts, always took the role of leading lady and gave Mr. Ullstein the male role. Mrs. Jarz read all other female parts. When Mr. Yoshoka was in town, he read the villain. The Czech boarder, after much prompting, agreed to participate and did assorted parts. I never rose above messenger. Once I was the chorus. Father refused to read a single line but attended every session.

We read Kleist, Lessing, Schiller, Goethe, and Shakespeare. *Othello* was the highlight. In keeping with the play's exotic setting, Mr. Yoshoka supplied everyone with a kimono, except for Mrs. Ullstein who, as Desdemona, wore a white nightgown. Halfway through Schiller's *Maria Stuart* something awful happened. Late one afternoon, two Gestapo men came to arrest the Czech boarder. When they entered his room, he jumped out of the window and killed himself.

We never read again.

In a recent speech, Goebbels had promised the citizens of Berlin that their city would be the first to be free of Jews. "I give you my solemn word," he had said. The Gestapo went to work. They arrested Jews in the streets in broad daylight; they came at night and forced them out of their apartments. Some said they were being resettled. No one ever heard from those who left. Many Jews killed themselves rather than wait to be taken away. A friend of Father's drowned himself in the Spree; an aunt of Mrs. Jarz stuck her head in the oven; another relative slashed her wrist.

Petrified that the Gestapo might come, I was afraid to go to sleep. I had nightmares. Sometimes I dreamed we were back in Osterburg with my sisters, and when I woke up it was worse than before I had gone to sleep because nothing had changed. I thought of Shanghai. Father had received a letter from Uncle Albert, who indeed had made it across Siberia, saying life in Shanghai was good and he was playing bridge every afternoon. But we were trapped. The police, the Gestapo, the concierge, everyone knew where we lived. It was just a question of time.

"Please," I pleaded with Mrs. Jarz, "save us."

Mrs. Jarz threw her arms around me. "Oh my God," she cried, "poor lamb." Her own future was uncertain.

Several days later, Mr. Ullstein called me into his room, where I found Father and Mrs. Jarz.

"Listen carefully," said Mr. Ullstein. "Mr. Yoshoka has been recalled to Japan. On his way, he has offered to take you to Zurich. The only way he can get you across the border is as his wife. He'll get the necessary papers. It's pro forma, of course. Once in Zürich he will place you in a boarding school."

I turned fire red. A bride at 13! I was flattered that the adults paid so much attention to me. What an honor. Would Mr. Yoshoka drive a Mercedes, I wondered. Would people address me as Madame? Switzerland. It was the ultimate dream. They spoke German in Zurich without being Germans. I longed to go back to school. I would study hard. My thoughts were racing.

I looked at Father.

"We have to do what's best for you," he said averting his eyes. "This may be your last chance."

My last chance? What about him? What was he talking about?

Did he think I would go by myself? Life without Father was unthinkable. The very thought made me ill. Goebbels could scream as much as he wanted; I didn't care. There was no way that I would go.

Several days later, Mr. Yoshoka left for Japan. In my room was a bouquet of red roses.

Next, Hitler decreed that Jews had to wear a yellow star when going outside. In case people didn't know what the star meant, it had "Jew" written on it.

I made my star detachable with snaps and removed it the minute I left our neighborhood.

The Ammunition Factory
March 1942-February 1943

Maybe I should have married Mr. Yoshoka after all. I could have been eating chocolate in Switzerland instead of working in a factory in Berlin. I hated the long hours, the noise, the monotony, and the stench. I complained to Father.

"Don't talk nonsense," he said. "We are lucky to have been included in the labor force. With every able-bodied German fighting on the fronts, they need Jewish people to work in factories to supply the German army with ammunition. It might protect us from being deported."

"At least for now," he added. "Be grateful."

Much as I tried to be grateful, I couldn't develop any enthusiasm. The factory I was assigned to was located in Kreuzberg, Berlin's most dismal neighborhood. The people here lived in barrack-like buildings connected by dingy courtyards with laundry hanging from filthy windows. The factory was all but hidden in the last building of those courtyards.

My shift started at six o'clock in the morning and ended at six o'clock in the evening. Father, who was assigned to another factory, worked the night shift. Taking the same subway at different hours from opposite directions, I always looked to catch a glimpse of Father as our trains rattled passed. In a way, I envied him the night shift. At least he didn't have to contend with those nightly air raids. In the beginning, I would get up like everybody else in the pension, get hastily dressed, and walk down to the cellar into our shelter, the one on the left, assigned to Jews.

To make it cozy, Mrs. Jarz had hung pictures on the walls, put rugs on the stone floor, and installed several cots with blankets. There were books, candles, an oil lamp in case the lights went out, water, and crackers that were so hard that Mr. Ullstein suggested they were leftovers from former sailing-vessel days.

But, having to get up before dawn, I didn't bother. Air raids and bombs notwithstanding, I stayed in bed. Often, I didn't even wake up.

When I got to work, I changed clothes, punched in, and started working. Six days a week. I worked on a machine that polished screws the size of my pinky nail. I attached an unpolished screw to a spindle, pressed a knob that set the screw spinning while oil trickled onto the screw to keep it from getting hot. The oil was black, thick, and rancid. Its odor settled on my hair, my clothes, and my skin. I was required to polish a thousand screws an hour.

All around me other machines operated, spitting out metal objects similar to my screws. I kept myself awake by singing loudly; nobody could hear because of the deafening noise. I belted out the latest hit songs and snippets of operettas.

Ralph, who was in charge of refilling the screw bins, heard me singing.

"You have a lovely voice," he shouted into my ears. "You could become a singer."

I told him I wanted to become a pianist.

He said he loved classical music and had this fantasy of becoming a conductor. He was a young, good-looking guy with a mass of dark, curly hair. Like everyone on the floor, except for the supervisors, Ralph was Jewish. We took lunch together, sitting on the fire escape, away from the stench.

He wanted to know what books I had read lately.

"Lately? I am too tired. I barely make it to work."

Ralph shook his head.

"Nonsense. Just because you work twelve hours in a factory doesn't mean you have to lose track of who you are. Train yourself. You need less sleep and more stimulation. Since this is all mechanical, it gives you plenty of time to follow your own thoughts."

He gave me a book by Herman Hesse. "I'd be interested to hear what you think."

He really cared. He spent more and more time next to my machine, pretending to fix it. He smiled when I told him that Liszt was my favorite composer and my dream was to play his second piano concerto.

"Very romantic," he said. "The composers to consider are the three B's: Bach, Beethoven, and Brahms"

He was appalled that I didn't know who Bach was.

"Tell you what," he said. "Tomorrow after work, we'll buy a Bach recording, go to my house, and listen. You are in for a treat!"

He lowered his voice: "Listening to Bach makes everything all right."

As agreed, we met outside the factory after our shift and took the trolley to Alexander Platz, which was way out of our neighborhood. When we reached Alexander Platz, we detached our stars.

"Wait across the street," said Ralph. "No point for the two of us to go into the store."

I waited, wondering where Ralph lived and what his parents were like. At any rate, I couldn't stay long. As it was, my coming home late would get me into plenty of trouble. The wait seemed endless. The three B's, I realized, could just as well be called the three F's, German composers forbidden to Jews. What a dumb thing having agreed to come here with Ralph. It simply wasn't worth it.

I was debating whether to enter the store and tell Ralph to

forget it when he emerged, flanked by two SS men. When Ralph struggled to free himself, the SS men pushed him against the wall and kicked his face. Ralph never looked in my direction, not even when they dragged him into a van. Then they were gone.

A small crowd had gathered.

"Hey, what happened?"

"Must be a Jew or something," said a woman.

"Bloody Jew," another woman said. "Serves him right. Soon they'll all be gone. Goebbels said so."

By the time I got home, Father had already gone to work. Mrs. Jarz threw her arms around me.

"My goodness," she cried, "we thought something had happened to you!

"Come, I've saved you some tripe."

I shook my head. "I have an upset stomach," I said. "I'd rather go to sleep."

In the night, I heard some commotion. Thinking it was an air raid, I went back to sleep. But in the morning I learned that Father's left hand had been caught into the welding machine. He had lost three fingers. Mrs. Jarz said she had given him a sleeping pill and he was resting now.

I tiptoed into his room. Father was snoring; his hand was bandaged. I was afraid to touch him.

"I'm going to work now," I whispered.

Standing in front of the machine, I couldn't bear the smell. The screws came tumbling down, forming one big mountain. The spindle rotated like crazy and started to smoke. Looking around, I found a wrench and banged it down on the machine with all my might. Then I sat on the stool. Within seconds, the full force of supervisors came running down the aisle.

"Saboteur! Jewish warmonger! Swine!" they shouted. "You'll pay for this!"

One of them grabbed me by the arm and marched me past the rows of machines. My coworkers bent their heads, not wishing to look. We walked down the corridor, into the elevator, up a flight of stairs in total silence. Knowing what the punishment for sabotage was, I tried not to think about it. Opening a door with a sign that said "Private keep out," the foreman pushed me into the room. Four men sat around a table, shouting. They didn't bother to look up.

"You heard me," said one of them. "I cannot promise making this week's quota if my people don't get paid by tomorrow."

I noticed he was the only one without a party button or the SS insignia on his work outfit.

"You mean there isn't anyone in this goddamn place who doesn't know how to add two and two together," one of them snickered.

"That's what I've been trying to tell you ever since you transferred the bookkeeper ... nobody."

The speaker sounded bored. Looking in our direction he asked brusquely,

"What do you want?"

I wasn't sure who he was addressing.

"I know how to do payroll," I blurted out. It came out just like that. I surprised myself.

There was a dead silence; everybody stared at me. I wanted to disappear into the ground. The angry man laughed.

"Shit," he said. He turned to the others. "Why not? We have nothing to lose. Let's try her."

Nobody said a word.

"Krause," said the man, "what are you staring at? Don't you have work to do? Get back to your station."

Turning to me, he asked me for my name and ID number.

"Where did you say you learned bookkeeping?"

"In school."

"Are you pulling my leg?"

"No, no. I swear."

He scribbled something on a piece of paper and handed it to me.

"Here's your pass. Come to my office tomorrow morning at seven. Fourth floor. My name is Runge."

Going home I felt like the miller's daughter who had been asked to spin straw into gold. Father was running a fever; still sedated, but his eyes were open. I told him about my promotion but did not mention anything about the sabotage. Father was already suspicious.

"There must be a dozen women on your floor who are qualified. How come he asked you?"

I shrugged my shoulders. "You know how they are—perverse, unpredictable. You said so yourself. I really need help figuring out how to do this job."

Father shook his head. "I don't know what this world is coming to. It takes years to become a bookkeeper. This is a real dilemma."

The next morning I found Mr. Runge's office, a glass enclosed booth that overlooked two wings of the factory: one with heavy machinery, operated by German women, Turks, and Bulgarians; the other with manual laborers, among them Jews with special privileges.

"So," said Mr. Runge. "How old did you say you are?"

"Eighteen."

"Come on, don't give me that."

"Sixteen," I ventured.

"And where exactly did you learn your clerical skills?"

"No place. That was a lie."

Mr. Runge slapped his thighs.

"That's a good one," he laughed. "I figured something like that. You certainly have spunk."

He looked around.

"I am surrounded by assholes."

He sighed. "There isn't one intelligent person in this entire place. Ass kissers that's who they are."

Doing the payroll wasn't all that complicated. With the help of an adding machine, I calculated each person's weekly pay based on the number of hours he or she had worked. I enjoyed handling the cash and prided myself in putting the exact amount of money into each person's envelope.

I stayed on as Mr. Runge's assistant for several months, answering the phone, opening his mail, arranging appointments, and doing the payroll. When Mr. Runge authorized me to copy his signature, I granted sick leaves and approved early departures. Everyone paid me the utmost respect in spite of the fact that I was the only Jew on this floor.

Some women had a crush on Mr. Runge and asked me if they could see him privately. Among them Miss Küstler, who always wore a swastika pin, nagged me the most. She had bulging eyes and crooked teeth, and I didn't blame Mr. Runge for imploring me to get her off his back. He called her a stupid cow and said he wished someone would push her down the elevator shaft.

I couldn't very well tell her that and made all kinds of excuses. One day, she cornered me in the ladies room.

"Don't think I don't know what's going on between the two of you," she said. "You won't get away with it; I promise you that."

It was too stupid to tell Mr. Runge. I liked him. He was extremely kind. To keep me from being bored, he had installed a radio under my desk with a hidden switch in case somebody was coming. He gave me cod-liver oil for my frostbitten fingers, saying it would help my circulation. He brought food: sausages, eggs, lard, and butter. His family owned a goose farm in the Sudentengau where Mr. Runge had grown up. He showed me pictures of his wife and little boy who had been born since he came to Berlin. I told him about Father and Mrs. Jarz.

Every day, I found some present in my drawer: a flashlight, candles, soap, shaving cream, tobacco, tea, and chocolate—items from the black market.

My office was warm, well lit, and soundproof. I looked forward to going to work. Father was better again, although those three fingers were gone for good. He said it didn't bother him, except that he now could tell the weather because his stumps started to itch before approaching rain. At the factory, they had put him on day shift, sorting polished parts by sizes.

One morning, Mr. Runge arrived late. He shuffled the papers on his desk, rearranging his pencils and drummed his fingers. He cleared his throat a few times.

"I have bad news," he finally said. "Tonight, the Gestapo is rounding up all Jews left in Berlin. They'll pick them up from their homes, places of work, in the streets."

He paused.

"Your father is a smart man," he continued. "If by chance he has made plans for you to go into hiding, you have to go now."

My heart skipped a few beats. Did he suspect that we did have a plan and were waiting for the right moment to carry it out?

Our plan had been masterminded by Mrs. Jarz thanks to my constant pleading to save us from being deported. When our situation became unbearable, we were to go to the apartment of Mr. and Mrs. Kraus in the suburb of Karlshorst. Lizzy Kraus was the sister of Mrs. Jarz's gentile husband; she and her husband Karl were devout Christians who said it was their duty to practice what their religion preached. Father and I didn't know them well. We had met them once or twice at the home of Mrs. Jarz's other relatives, the Wagenführs, who owned a hairdressing salon on Kurfürstendam. Mrs. Wagenführ was a stout woman with watery blue eyes. She wore her blond tresses in a crown on top of her head, imitating Alda von Schira, the Nazi symbol of German motherhood. The similarity stopped there because Mrs. Wagenführ didn't have children. Instead she had furs: sable, mink, fox, beaver, lamb, and ermine—coats, jackets, muffs, and shawls. They had all been given to her by former Jewish clients for safekeeping till their return. Meanwhile, Mrs. Wagenführ wore these furs as if they were hers.

Lizzy Kraus, I was sure, would never do such a thing. In fact, it was hard to imagine her in furs. Mild mannered and simply dressed, she seemed ill at ease with her rich relatives. Mrs. Wagenführ called her the church mouse.

But it was Lizzy Kraus, the "church mouse," and her husband who offered to hide us in their home.

I was elated, but Father initially refused

"It is wonderful that there are such people," he told Mrs. Jarz. "I am deeply touched, but I can't risk their lives for the sake of ours. If anybody would even suspect that they are hiding us, they would be shot."

"They offered," ventured Mrs. Jarz. "It might mean something to them we may not understand."

"I never asked for this," said Father. "Hitler rules half of Europe, and there is no end in sight. I'm resigned to my fate."

"Resigned? Resigned to being hauled off to some terrible, unknown place?" I was not resigned.   I had always counted on Father to protect me. What happened to him? Mrs. Jarz thought it had to do with having lost three fingers in the accident at the factory.

"It changed him," she said.

That, I thought, was all the more reason for him to go underground. It would be peaceful at the Kraus's. Father could rest. He could read, put Mr. Kraus's stamp collection in order, play chess. But Father was adamant.

And then, just when things seemed hopeless, the Russian Army came to my rescue. After years of retreating from the Germans, they picked themselves up, broke the Stalingrad siege, recaptured Rostov, and gave the Germans a beating. For the first time. the German Army was on the run, and the tide of the war seemed to be turning.

Mr. Kraus came and asked Father to reconsider.

"A thousand years!" said Mr. Kraus. "At most I give them another two. Surely, you can afford to wait that long. We will celebrate the collapse of the Third Reich together. I am saving a cognac for that occasion."

Father threw up his hands. "I am outnumbered."

It was the first time I saw him smile again.

To ensure the success of our hiding, a carefully laid plan was worked out.

Foremost was the matter of food, since the Kraus's could not feed four people on the rations of two. Mrs. Kraus's youngest brother promised to provide most of what was needed. He had been the laughingstock of the family, a drifter who lived in a shabby bungalow on the outskirts of Berlin. He raised chicken and rabbits, grew his own vegetables, cultivated mushrooms and orchids. It was rumored that he had been a Bolshevik and that he could not get work for that reason.

"Nonsense!" said Mrs. Wagenführ. "He was and will always be a bum."

"Don't listen to my sister," he told Father. "I give you may word; I'll not let you starve."

The Wagenführs too made a promise. They agreed to finance whatever had to be bought on the black market. "Christian charity," they called it. Just in case that charity would collapse, Father had given them his valuable coin collection to sell, if needed.

Mr. Runge looked at me.

"Where is your father at this moment?"

"At the factory." I bit my lower lip until it bled.

Mr. Runge scratched his head, muttering to himself. He took a sheet of paper and wrote a brief note to which he affixed a number of seals.

"That ought to do it." He sounded pleased.

He handed me the note.

"Go to your father's factory and show this note to the security guards. It instructs them to release your father from work and have him accompany you."

I looked at the note. It ordered father's presence at such and such a place without fail. The matter was urgent.

"But ... but ...," I was so flustered, I stuttered.

"Think of it as a joke," said Mr. Runge. "You'll have to sound authoritative. Shout; threaten them. That's the only thing these dumbkopfs understand."

I stared at Mr. Runge in disbelief. Did he really think I could pull this off? Mr. Runge didn't know Father. Father never acted on impulse. He would call my name and ask a hundred questions. I could possibly handle the security guards. Father was another matter. I would have to come up with something clever, slip in a word only he would understand. I got lost in thought.

Mr. Runge encouraged me.

"Come on now. You can do it. I know you have balls. Remember how we met?" He chuckled.

"Write yourself a dismissal slip and leave."

He raised his hand in a salute. Swiveling his chair around, he turned his back.

He did not say good-bye.

At father's factory, I presented the note to the guards at the gate and told them to hurry. Studying the official-looking document, they did not question my authority. Father came downstairs. He was upset and kept on saying "What's wrong?" I was so nervous, I could have slapped him. He wanted to go back and get his coat.

"No coat," I screamed. "There is no time."

I grabbed Father by the arm and pulled him away. The guards actually saluted as we left. When we turned the corner, I quickened the pace.

"Wait," Father whispered. "What's going on?"

No one was watching. The street was empty. I removed Father's star and threw it into the sewer. Then I told him the news. He was confused and talked about getting our things.

"Forget it, "I said. "We have to go now, this minute and take the train to Karlshorst."

We stood in the street arguing. Finally, Father agreed.

"It's best if we don't go together," he said. "You go first." He thought for a moment. "Maybe you could warn Uncle Sigie and Aunt Paula. Who knows? They too may have made arrangements. What do you think?"

I thought warning them was pretty dumb, but I was so anxious to have Father go ahead, I agreed.

"Be careful," he said. He took my hand. "Do only what can be done safely."

Uncle Sigie and Aunt Paula lived in the Hansa district. It took me twenty minutes to get there. When I arrived at their house I saw a truck. It was an open vehicle, crowded with Jews. Others stood patiently in line. I saw little Herbie but vainly looked for his parents. They must still be in their respective factories. At four years old, Herbie was advanced for his age. He had to be since there was no one to look after him while his parents worked. He was proud of his independence. "I know how to tie my shoe laces." Now he stood alone, wearing a red sweater. Had he chosen it? Where were his hat and gloves? I thought I should go and protect him. Instead, I stood frozen at a safe distance, hoping he would not see me. An elderly woman put her arm around him. She would take care of him, surely.

I turned away. It was cold. I thought of the time ahead. Going into hiding. I couldn't imagine what it would be like.

At Lehrter station, I stepped up to the ticket office.

"Karlshorst. One way, please."

Hiding in Berlin
February 1943–June 1944

Karlshorst, a suburb of Berlin, consisted of rows of identical four-story houses occupied by minor functionaries and retirees. The apartment of Mr. and Mrs. Kraus—I called them Uncle Karl and Aunt Lizzy—was on the third floor. It had a bedroom, living/dining room, a kitchen, a pantry, a small sewing room, and a den. The den became Father's and my room. The room was long and narrow with a glass-paneled door to a balcony. When we moved in, Aunt Lizzy covered the door with a thick curtain, thereby putting the room into permanent blackout.

The room had a sofa, two armchairs, a footstool, coffee table, sideboard with Delft china, a book case, and a small writing desk. Father slept on the sofa. I slept on the floor on a roll-up mattress. Father snored.

The bookcase contained *The Big Brockhaus* (an encyclopedia); a World Atlas, novels by Lagerlof, Söderman, Thomas Mann, and Tolstoy; plays by Ibsen; poetry of Heine and Möricke; and a limited edition of Busch's *Max und Moritz*. There were stacks of technical manuscripts and pamphlets on electric power, which was Mr. Kraus's field. There were prints of Leonardo's "Head of Christ," Dürer's "Apocalypse," Millet's "Angelus," and a series of

Persian miniatures, which were the pride of Aunt Lizzy, who once dreamed of studying art history.

The *Brockhaus* was a revelation. It contained all knowledge from A to Z and had wonderful illustrations. Starting with Aachen and Zwickhaus, I decided to tackle it from the beginning and the end at the same time, hoping that the war would be over way before I'd reached the middle.

Father devised a routine. In the morning we exercised: stretches, push-ups, knee-bends—movements that couldn't be heard on the floor below. Next, I helped Aunt Lizzy with household chores. Although we never had visitors, Aunt Lizzy kept the place as if she was expecting the Pope. Sweeping and dusting took half the morning. Each day there was an additional task: I waxed the floors on Monday and polished the silver Tuesday. The crystal kept behind a glass-enclosed cupboard and never used was washed Wednesdays. Thursdays I ironed. On Fridays, I combed the fringes of the rugs.

After that, I did homework: geography, history, and French, all assigned and supervised by Father. I also wrote a novel, which I lifted largely from other books. In the afternoon, I peeled carrots, potatoes, and turnips in preparation for dinner.

Food wasn't important to Aunt Lizzy. If she could have had her way, she would have traded her food ration for cigarettes and coffee. Except for Sundays, our meals were always the same: vegetable stews of carrots, kale, turnips, or cabbage. Sundays we had a bit of meat, gravy, potatoes, and a homemade pound cake. Half of the pound cake was wrapped and stored in the pantry, to be served slice by slice during the rest of the week. When the two of them went to prayer meetings, I went into the pantry and sneaked a tiny piece.

Father spent most of his time examining and evaluating Uncle Karl's stamps. He placed them in books and catalogued them according to countries. He loved those stamps and got excited over watermarks, perfect edges, and first editions. He urged me to take an interest. I didn't care. It was enough that Father insisted I play chess.

Father had been a champion player, taught by a Grand Master.

"Chess is an excellent discipline," Father said. "Like Latin, but more useful."

To me, chess was about as useful as stilt walking, but less fun. Having to sit for hours and concentrating with Father breathing down my neck made me so nervous, I thought I'd break out into hives. Father explained the role of the different pieces: the pawns, knights, rooks, bishops and how they moved. Their sole purpose was to protect the king and queen. To make it easier, he played without the queen; later he forfeited his rooks; then the bishops, down to a couple of pawns. Gradually, I improved. I started to enjoy the game, and winning became a challenge. Uncle Karl, a pretty good chess player himself, joined us in the game. On Father's birthday, I beat both of them. Father beamed.

"Best present you could give me."

In the evening, Father and Uncle Karl listened to the BBC. After the news broadcast they rolled out the war chart on which they marked the advancing or retreating armies with pins: red-tipped for the Russians, green for the British, yellow for the Italians, and black for the Germans. The news was good: the red-tipped pins moved from Smolensk to Kiev, while green pins appeared in Naples. Father and Uncle Karl had served in the First World War. Both had been decorated with the AK 1, the Iron Cross, for the bravery shown in the battle field. They talked about it as if it was yesterday, although now they cheered for the other side. Aunt Lizzy retired to the bedroom. I stayed up and darned socks.

Aunt Lizzy started and ended her days with prayers.

"Why does she pray so much," I asked Father. "What's her religion?"

"Why don't you ask her," said Father.

One day I did.

"We are Theosophists," she said. She explained that Theosophy was a form of mysticism that reconciled the existence of an all-powerful and all-good God with the presence of evil in the world.

I didn't know what she was talking about.

She smiled and took my hand.

"Dear child. Isn't it wonderful that God's mysterious ways have brought you and your Father to our house?"

Despite her strange ways, I liked Aunt Lizzy. She had traveled, studied art, knew a lot about history, and loved music. In the dining room stood her black upright. She said she hadn't played for a while, and it was out of tune. To please me, she occasionally sat down and played: Bach's two-part inventions, Handel's "Harmonious Blacksmith," and early Haydn sonatas. Not used to an audience, she blushed and apologized for her shortcomings. How I longed to play! Of course that was out of the question, since for all and intents purposes Father and I could not make a sound.

But I daydreamed a lot. Usually about giving a concert to an enraptured audience. The music just popped into my head. Pieces I knew: Schumann's "Kinderscenen," Schubert's "Moments Musicaux" or "Wanderer Fantastie," Beethoven sonatas, and Mozart. I always was the soloist. At other times, I imagined living with the artists. I prevented Schumann from throwing himself into the Rhein and, at other times, was the mistress of Franz Liszt. I also staged some opera performances, although I had never seen a single one.

That's how I injured myself one evening. I was washing the dishes while deep into performing Beethoven's "Moonlight Sonata." I broke a glass and cut the place between my thumb and forefinger. The wound didn't stop bleeding. Aunt Lizzy took me into her arms. "Don't be frightened, child. It's only a flesh wound. You'll feel better in no time."

Father thought I might need some stitches.

"Out of the question." Uncle Karl shook his head. "We cannot take her to a doctor."

Having been a paramedic during the war, he sterilized my

wound, covered it with gauze, and bandaged it. Father made a sling from a kitchen towel and told me to keep my arm upright. Aunt Lizzy treated me to a piece of salami and made chamomile tea.

While Aunt Lizzy found solace in prayer, I discovered poetry, especially the poems of Eduard Möricke:

> *Frühling lässt sein blaues Band*
> *Wieder flattern durch die Lüfte,*
> *Süsse, wohlbekannte Düfte*
> *Streifen ahnungsvoll das Land.*
> *Veilchen träumen schon*
> *Wollen balde kommen.*
> *Horch von fern ein leiser Harfenton!*
> *Frühling, ja du bist's!*
> *Dich hab' ich vernommen!*
> Once again, spring weaves its charm
> gaily through the breezes;
> Sweet, well-known aromas
> fill the land.
> Violets dream of their return.
> Hark, from far the sound of a harp!
> Spring, yes it's you!
> I anticipate your coming!

I loved these poems; they comforted me during the ever-increasing nightly air-raids.

Father thrived on the air-raids and referred to the bombers as our liberators. "Look at the spectacle," he cried, pointing to the gigantic red and green circles which exploded in the sky like fireworks. Father said they marked the targets for the bombers. I closed my eyes and covered my ears as bombs hissed through air and crashed into houses, which exploded into flames. I crouched in the corner of the room and belted out Möricke's poems.

One night, a bomb hit so close to our house that the shock

wave threw me flat on the floor. The windows blew out, and our balcony disappeared into thin air. I was afraid Father might have been swept away. When he appeared, I rushed into his arms, sobbing.

"That was a close one," he said, shaking off the debris.

After the all-clear alarm was sounded, the building was roped off because it was feared it might collapse. All tenants went to the nearby high school until other arrangements could be made. Father and I tagged along. In the confusion no one cared who we were or where we came from. We were given cots and blankets in the gym of the high school; a soup kitchen had been set up. Teachers issued temporary identification cards and food ration coupons. It was the perfect chance for us to become legitimate. We explained that we had just been bombed out of our house in Berlin and had asked our friends in Karlshorst to stay with them. Father rose to the occasion and said his name was William "after the Kaiser." When they asked him if he had lost his fingers in the war, Father said "yes," which earned him double food rations. I became Gisela Müller.

After ten days in the shelter, our house was declared safe and the four of us moved back. There was only one hitch: at sixteen I had to attend school or go to work. Father, with his new status of war invalid, was excused from work. But in order not to arouse suspicion from the neighbors, I needed to leave the house on school days. Five days a week, I left the house at eight o' clock and rode the commuter train to Berlin. The walk to the station took fifteen minutes; the ride to town took another thirty-five. That left me with six hours to kill. In the beginning, I was elated over my new freedom, but Berlin was half destroyed—even the animals in the zoo had been evacuated—and, without a purpose, what could I do? I counted on air raids, since they enabled me to seek refuge in the bomb shelters and kill time. Occasionally, I treated myself to a movie, although I felt uncomfortable sitting by myself in the dark theater in the middle of the day. Occasionally,

I went to the Pergamon, one of the few museums still standing. Often, I just rode the trolleys.

Twice a month, I took the train to the outskirts of Berlin to pick up coal and food from Aunt Lizzy's brother, Hans Jarz. His place was decorated with manifestos, old newspapers, and posters of Lenin and Trotsky.

"Have some bread and lard," Mr. Jarz always urged. "You are as skinny as a stick."

But I knew that, together with the bread and the lard, I would have to listen to Mr. Jarz lecture about Karl Marx. I couldn't wait to leave. I thanked him for the coal, stashed away the eggs, chicken, and rabbit giblets he gave me, and paid him as instructed by Father.

The winter of 1944 was bitter cold. To seek shelter from a snowstorm one afternoon, I entered the Marienkirche (St. Mary's Church) at the Kaiser-Wilhelm Street. Someone was playing the organ. I took a seat in one of the pews. When the organist emerged, he was startled to see me.

"Was that Bach?" I asked.

"Yes."

Bach. I was overcome with joy.

"I want to learn to play the organ," I said. "Can you teach me?"

The organist smiled. With his gold-rimmed glasses and gray mutton chops, he looked like a professor.

"You can't be more than five feet tall," he said. "You will fall off the organ bench."

"I'm five feet one and very agile."

I mentioned that I played the piano and was a fairly good sight reader.

"Why the organ?" he asked.

I couldn't explain.

"We'll give it a try," he said. "When are you free?"

"Always," I wanted to say, but I knew better. "Tuesdays and Thursdays," I said.

Due to an air raid, I was one and a half hours late for the

arranged appointment. The organist was still there. We went up to the organ loft where I hoisted myself up on the organ bench as instructed.

It was the beginning of a new life.

The organist—I called him maestro and never asked his name—gave me the key to the organ loft so that I could come and go as I pleased. He arranged for the church attendant—a deaf-mute—to pump the bellow whenever I requested. Twice a week, the maestro gave me lessons. By pulling a few stops, I could produce sounds that muffled sirens and exploding bombs. The organ loft became my sanctuary.

The reaction at home was mixed. Aunt Lizzy said God was showing me the way; Father felt uncomfortable about my spending so much time in church; Uncle Karl launched into a long explanation of the principle of the bellow.

I joined the church choir where, for want of men, the maestro assigned me to the tenor section. When we performed Brahms's "German Requiem" with a full orchestra and soloists, I was so overcome with joy I missed my cue and came in four bars late. I was the only one who didn't have relatives or friends come to the concert. But everyone knew that I was an orphan, originally from Schleswig-Holstein, staying with hard-working, distant relatives.

Leaving the church one late afternoon, I ran into Miss Küstler, the Nazi woman from my former factory whom Mr. Runge had called a stupid cow. I started to run.

"Catch her! Grab her. Jew! Police!"

I raced down the Neuer Markt with what seemed half of Berlin following. An air raid might have saved me but, for once, the sirens remained silent. A Hitler Youth caught up with me and held me. I stood panting. Miss Küstler appeared momentarily, a look of triumph on her face.

"Miss High and Mighty," she snarled, "I told you I would get even with you."

The crowd parted to make way for the arriving policeman.

"What have we got here?"

"A Jew," cried Miss Küstler. "A dirty, filthy Jew who tried to escape the law."

"A Jew?" The policeman looked perplexed. "I thought they were all gone."

"Are you doubting my word?" shouted Miss Küstler. "I am a party member."

"I'll take her to the police station," explained the police man to the crowd. "They will hand her over to the Gestapo."

"I'll be checking up on you." said Miss Küstler. "I want the full report."

The policeman took my arm.

"You are not going to cause any trouble," he said. "Otherwise I'll have to handcuff you."

I barely listened because there were two things I had to do before reaching the police station: dispose of my false ID and call Father. The first proved quiet simple. Pretending to trip as we crossed the street, I dropped my identification card into the gutter. Calling Father was another matter.

I studied the policeman. Portly, with red cheeks and a snub nose, he looked like a family man. I decided to risk it.

"I have to make a call," I said, holding my breath.

He didn't object. We stopped at a street phone. I deposited a *Groschen*, shielding the number I was dialing. Aunt Lizzy answered the phone.

"I am in a rush," I blurt. "Please put Father on,"

When I heard Father's voice, I almost lost heart.

"Väti," I said, trying to control the tremor in my voice, "please listen and don't interrupt. I got caught."

Before I could continue, Father cut in.

"Where are you, my child? I'll come immediately to join you."

"Don't, please," I begged. "I'll be alright, but only if you promise one thing: Swear you'll remain where you are. Do this for me. It will give me strength. I'll hold out as long as I can feel that you are all right."

I paused for a moment. I could hear Father breathing.

"Väti?" I heard sobs.

"Will you give me your word?"

"You have my word."

I placed the telephone back into the receiver. My hand was shaking.

The Longest Day
June 6, 1944

When I saw the SS man walk toward me, whip in hand and German shepherd at his side, I thought: "Oh God, I'm done for." I was sure he would ask me about Father's whereabouts and insist I tell him. I had no illusions about how I would bear up under torture.

"A Jew?" the SS man seemed surprised.

Was that a question? I wondered.

I was so nervous, I couldn't think straight.

The SS man shuffled through some papers on his desk. He barely paid attention.

"Where were you hiding all this time?"

"Many places," I said, stalling for time.

He looked up briefly but didn't seem to care. Questions about Father never came up. In fact, the SS man seemed bored. When the phone rang, he grabbed the receiver. Listening to the party on the other end, he laughed uproariously. Even the dog pricked up his ears.

"Man, what a story," he shouted. "Wait till Herman hears about this. I'll be right down."

He dismissed me with a wave of his hand. "Take her away," he said to the two wardens who had respectfully remained in the back of the room. The wardens, an elderly man and a woman, were eager to talk.

"This is part of a hospital," they explained. "In this wing, they used to keep the mental patients." They said they missed their mental cases. "We took good care of them."

I wanted to ask where the mental patients were now, but just then, we entered a room which, I assumed, was going to be my quarters. A middle-aged couple came to greet me. They had been here for almost four weeks.

"We thought we might be the only Jews left in Berlin." They seemed disappointed by my arrival. They explained that the Gestapo was waiting to round up ten Jews before a transport to a camp would be worthwhile.

"We had hoped this might take forever," they added.

They introduced themselves as Dr. Irene and Dr. Magnus Orenstein and said they were both psychiatrists. I told them I didn't know what that was. They were shocked.

"How is it possible that a girl like you should be so ignorant?"

"I haven't been to school for quite some time," I stammered.

"You realize," said Dr. Magnus Orenstein, "subconsciously you wished to be caught."

I had never heard such rubbish in my life and wondered if I had landed in a loony bin. Maybe the doctor was a left over mental case. The only other inmate was a young woman, Katja. She spoke the most horrible German.

"Yiddish," said the woman doctor. "An Eastern Jew, not one of us."

The Eastern Jew had bleached hair. I understood she was a hairdresser from Romania.

The room contained benches, a table, side cupboards, and sleeping cots, which were lines up against either side of the wall. Beyond the heavy bars on the window, I could see a garden; the chestnut trees were in full bloom. Before I had time to settle in, the woman warden came to fetch me, saying the house doctor wanted to see me.

"Is this part of the routine?" I asked as we went up the stairs.

"You never know around here," said the warden.

She knocked at a door, ushered me in, and left. I was alone with the doctor. Facing him, I could hardly believe my eyes. Dr. Kornbluth! Our Berlin dentist; a Jew like me and Father. What was he doing here?

"How nice to see a familiar face," he said. He took a cigarette out of a silver case, tapped the cigarette against the desk and fitted it into a black cigarette holder. For a moment it looked as if he was going to offer me one.

"I forgot how young you are," he said, snapping the case tight.

He seemed pleased at the encounter.

"How is your dear father?"

"Father is dead," I said, looking Dr. Kornbluth straight in the eyes. When you looked people straight in the eyes, I had learned, you could tell them anything and they believed you. That's how I had gotten false identification papers for me and Father after our hiding place had been bombed out and we had to give an explanation who we were and where we had come from.

"You are all by yourself then?" Dr. Kornbluth mumbled. He leaned forward.

"You are lucky." He lowered his voice. "I may be able to help you."

He moved from behind the desk, swinging himself on top, in front of me. He was as chubby as I remembered.

"You could remain here," he said. "Have your own room and come and go as you please. You will lack nothing: pocket money, clothing, and food. Good meals, I might add. Books. We have a well-stocked library and one of the best bomb shelters in town."

He paused.

"How does that sound?"

It sounded weird.

"I don't understand," I said.

He extinguished his cigarette and stretched out his hand.

"Think of it as a new life; a new you, free from worries and fears."

"Was this a trap?" I wondered

As if reading my mind, Dr. Kornbluth continued. "No need to worry. You'll have a new name and identity. With your looks, you would carry it off very well."

"What's the catch?" I asked.

"No catch. Just a little cooperation with the Gestapo."

"Like what?"

"Assist in finding the remaining Jews and other enemies of the State."

He made it sound like the most natural thing.

"These are tough times," he said. "Why end up in camp when you could have a future here?"

"Is that what you do?" I swallowed hard. "Turn people in?"

He let go of my hand.

"I am a dentist," he said. "That's what I do." This time he was not smiling.

"I know this is hard," he continued. "You don't have to decide this minute. But take my advice: be smart and grab this opportunity."

"No point being a martyr," he added, "particularly since you don't have to account to any one."

He rang for the warden.

"Once you have decided, tell the warden you wish to see me. Of course, I count on your discretion. Not a word to anyone."

How I longed to tell Father. He probably wouldn't believe me. That was the difficult part about being here; being so close to Father and not able to call him.

Two days later, our group was joined by an elderly man. He was wailing and crying, wringing his hands and beating his chest. When the doctors managed to calm him down, he told us he was from Poland. He said he had been a tailor and spoke five languages.

At night I heard him pray. The next day, he produced a miniature chess set. Dr. Magnus Orenstein rubbed his hands. "Set it up, my good man. By all means, let's go."

We took turns and when I beat both the tailor and Dr. Marcus, the doctor was impressed.

"Congratulations. Who taught you to play?"

I was about to tell him Father did, but caught myself.

"Friends," I said, close to tears.

Katja provided diversion by saying she read palms. The doctors said that this was gypsy hocus pocus and declined to participate. I was curious. Katja studied the inside of my left hand.

"I see bad times ahead," she muttered. "But, you have a long life line and, at the end, you'll triumph."

The tailor thrust out his hands. After a quick glance, Katja closed his palms.

"I can't concentrate anymore," she said. "Some other time."

We had just finished supper when the warden delivered another prisoner. He was young and so thin his trousers hung about him like rags. He spoke French. The doctors, who were quite fluent in that language, questioned him.

"He says his name is Guy and that he is not Jewish," they informed us.

At that, the tailor lost control. "Oy, oy," he cried. "If he isn't Jewish, he shouldn't be here. With him we are six; more than half the quota."

It was obvious that the Frenchman didn't want to be here either. He kept pacing up and down. Once he grabbed the window bars and tried to shake them. He begged everybody for a cigarette, as if people walked around with cigarettes in their pockets. When the lights were turned out, I heard him thrash about on his cot.

I couldn't sleep either and lay awake counting the church clock strike the hours. Toward morning, I heard birds chirping. I tiptoed over to the window and hoisted myself onto the window sill. There was a light breeze. Daybreak was coming. June. My favorite month because it had the longest days. Back in Osterburg, on midsummer night, the young people lit bonfires in the field. Holding hands with their sweethearts, they jumped over the fire, which bound them for life.

The warden came and took Guy. He never returned.

"He was probably a spy," said the tailor. "They probably shot him."

We settled into a routine. Except for the air raids, I felt quite comfortable. In fact, it was a relief not having to worry where to spend my days without arousing suspicion. Even the food was adequate. I too came to think that I might be here for a long, long time.

With the arrival of the two little girls everything changed. We waited all day for the children's parents, but they didn't come. The warden said she understood the children had been picked up crossing the border from Germany into Switzerland. The parents apparently had made it.

"How is that possible?" we wondered. "How could such a thing happen? Leaving the children behind?"

Everyone had a different reaction. Survival instinct, according to the doctors. Katja said perhaps the parents trusted in God. The tailor was only interested in numbers.

"Seven," he cried. "Now we are seven."

The girls told us their names were Tilly and Gaby. Holding up their fingers, they signaled they were four and five. They had sweet little faces, snub noses, and brown eyes as big as bing cherries. When they smiled, dimples appeared. Their hair was the color of honey. They wore identical outfits: blue, pleated skirts with suspenders fastened with mother-of-pearl buttons, short-sleeve white shirts with round collars, white ankle socks, and sturdy brown shoes.

They talked about mama and papa as if their parents had just left for a tea party. As the day went on they became worried and cried. To distract them I told them stories. Using two napkins, Katja and I made rag dolls for them.

By bedtime, the girls grew agitated and wanted their mama. I put two mattresses on the floor so that the three of us could be close.

"Don't get too involved," Dr. Irene advised me in the morning. "Under the circumstances it's not wise to form attachments."

I enjoyed taking care of the children. Katja helped; even the tailor cheered up and entertained them with songs. We formed a circle and danced, joined by Dr. Irene. Her husband stood by and clapped.

When the warden entered and clapped his hands, we thought he had joined in the fun.

"You'll be leaving first thing in the morning," he said. "Get your things ready."

We remained standing in the middle of the room, paralyzed.

"More, more!" The children wanted to dance.

"They said they needed ten people." Even Dr. Magnus was dumfounded. "And the children? Surely, the children will not be part of the transport."

"I'm only telling you what I was told," said the warden. "I think they need this room."

As far as getting ready, I didn't even have a toothbrush. Katja felt sorry for me.

"Would you like me to do your hair? It would give me pleasure."

She washed my hair with the water from the bucket in the bathroom we used to flush the toilets. At home, Minna had always washed my hair with rain water, saying it was the only water fit for my fine hair. Now Katja rolled strands of it around newspaper strips. The girls laughed. Dr. Irene was amused: "You look like a character out of Max and Moritz."

I told the girls that, tonight, they would be sleeping on their own cot and I would sleep on mine. To give them enough space, I had Tilly face one way and Gaby the other so that their feet were next to each others faces. They promptly tickled each others soles and only stopped giggling when the doctors told them to be quiet.

I lay curled up on my cot. Without the children next to me, I felt cold. The newspaper strips gave me a headache. I untied them and tossed them under my cot. A camp. Where would it be? And what would it be like? Since Tilly and Gaby were coming with us, they must have a nursery school there—an outdoor place with grass and trees.

I thought of Ruth and the songs she had taught me. "Red roses on the hillside; the wind in the mountains; I rejoice, I rejoice …" But when I came to "that the world is so beautiful," I couldn't go on. What was the matter with me? I had promised Father I would be strong, and here I was whimpering, feeling sorry for myself. I must get through the song. But, no matter how hard I tried, every time I came to the part about the beautiful world, my voice broke. Still struggling, I fell asleep.

Early in the morning, the seven of us boarded a police truck. I half expected to see Dr. Kornbluth. After a long ride, the vehicle deposited us at a freight depot. Gestapo men herded us toward a train and into an empty car. The air was stale; it smelled of horses. There was no place to sit.

After a while, I had to go to the bathroom. When I couldn't hold it any longer, I overcame my embarrassment and told the soldier who was guarding the door.

"Hi Willy," the soldier shouted to one of his buddies below. "The Jew girl has to piss."

He motioned for me to follow Willy. We walked around the train and stopped behind the first box car.

"Here." The soldier pointed to the ground.

"Here?"

"Where else? What do you want? The Kempinski?"

He turned his back and stood, legs apart, leaning on his rifle. I crouched down. I felt so humiliated, I couldn't squeeze a drop out.

"Ready?" the soldier turned around.

I shook my head.

"Hurry up," he said. "We don't have all day."

I stood up and pulled up my pants.

"The Americans have landed in Normandy."

"Did you say something?"

"The Americans have landed in Normandy." The soldier turned around. I looked at his face. It was that of a farm boy, not much older than I.

"Come on now. We can't stay here all day."

I didn't want to get up. I wanted to remain here, hidden behind the freight cars and wait for the Americans.

Back in the car, I found the doctors huddled in one corner. Dr. Magnus had his arms around his wife. She was shaking.

I kneeled besides them.

"The Americans have landed in Normandy," I whispered.

"Come on!"

"It's true, believe me."

"How do you know? Are you sure?"

"Yes."

"Darling," said the doctor. "Did you hear? The Americans have landed in Normandy. The war will be over soon."

I joined Katja and the little girls who were sprawled out in another corner. The train jolted. It moved forward and backward, then forward again. We were moving.

A New Beginning
Summer 1945

They made two mistakes at the hospital. According to the chart above my bed they listed my age as twelve and my profession as prostitute.

"Twelve," I thought, "I must be older than that."

I asked them what year this was. They said it was 1945. That made me eighteen and I told them. But I said nothing else.

The head of the clinic, a woman doctor, came to see me. "This is a civilian hospital in Hamburg," she said. "English soldiers brought you. The war is over."

I turned away from her.

"You have been here almost two months," the doctor continued. "You came with a truckload of prostitutes from a nearby detention camp. You had typhus and waved in and out of consciousness.

She hesitated for a moment. "You are the only girl the English had brought who did not have syphilis. I can't quite believe you're a prostitute. Who are you? Trust me."

I looked at her. Was she crazy? Here I was, nice and warm, and I should trust her? Maybe the war was over; maybe not. It would take a lifetime to ever trust a German again and another hundred years to trust a doctor.

She pointed to the number on my arm. "We thought there may be a chance that you are Jewish, although that seems unlikely. The English found a sealed freight car with Jews in a nearby in a tunnel. There were no survivors."

I wished she'd leave me alone.

I tried to remember the last camp. It consisted of a few shabby barracks, enclosed by barbed wire. No one seemed in charge. We stood and waited. The leader of our transport was debating with the camp commander. They slapped each other on the shoulder, laughing. The commander blew a whistle.

"Line-up. Criminals and whores to the right; Jews to the left."

"Jews forward march."

"Where to?" I thought. "There's no place left to go." I knew for sure that once outside the gate I would be walking to my death. I reversed my step and inched backward. I reached the last row of the remaining prisoners just as the Jews were marching out of camp.

The camp was a penal colony for social undesirables. Whores and criminals mingled easily. Supervision was lax. It would be a matter of minutes before my yellow star would give me away. I retreated to an empty upper bunk.

No living soul ever took her clothes off for fear that they might be stolen, but someone was bound to die during the night. Luck was on my side. I heard the familiar death rattle just below. I slipped down and stared at the open eyes of a skeleton of a girl who must have just died. I slipped her prison uniform with the black triangle over her head and exchanged it for mine. I didn't have the strength to leave my bunk after that

"You are getting stronger," said the doctor. "If, as you say, you are prostitute, I'll have to turn you over to a social worker."

The social worker was an elderly woman, plain and business-like. By that time, having gained some weight, I no longer looked twelve, and she was relieved to learn that I was an adult and not a child prostitute, although she had been willing to make allowances for it.

"The war did strange things," she said, "but this is all behind us. We will put you into a home for delinquents. You can learn a trade and make an honest living."

She made arrangements to meet me at the hospital on the day of my release within the next few days.

I'd met my first prostitutes in the Helmstedt camp infirmary, which consisted of a small, narrow room with an alcove for the attendant and two rows of triple bunk beds. Each one of them was occupied by three to four girls. They were horrible to look at—they lay open-eyed, wasted, mere shells. They had sores on their hands and large patches of fungus all over their bodies. Some were constantly drooling; others seemed paralyzed.

"What's the matter with them?" I asked the attendant.

She spat on the floor. "Syphilis, that's what; whores and pickpockets. They thought they were hot shit because they pilfered the church kitty or fucked some dumb bastard. I killed my old man with my own hands and went after my mother-in-law with an ax."

Balding, nearly toothless, she looked like a witch. "She'll eat me alive," I thought. Instead she treated me like a rare bird. I was her first Jew, she said. She fed me charcoal-broiled potato peels, spiced with coarse salt, and tried to educate me.

"There's no future in being a Jew. But, with your airs and education you'd make a good courtesan. There's a lot of money in it, and it is a good life. Listen to the whores. Dumb as they are, they can teach you the basics."

As it happened, I never got around to the basics because the Russian army was advancing and, once more, we were on the run. The attendant brought me a pair of shoes. "Leave the infirmary and go back to the Jewish barracks," she said. "I heard we are evacuating the camp."

She pointed to the bunks. "Who knows what they are going to do with these creatures."

I asked the head nurse for permission to walk around the town before my release. She discussed it with the staff, and they had no objections. I left wearing a clean hospital gown. A nurse lent me her shoes. I had no idea what I wanted to accomplish.

At the hospital they said this was Hamburg, but it could have been anyplace. The town was in shambles; nothing but ruins, rubble, and burned-out houses. Dragging myself halfway across a deserted square, I stopped and stared straight ahead. It was hot. I felt weak and had a mind to return to the hospital .I sat down and looked at this wasteland. Here and there people were poking around the ruins. The smell of the charred houses reminded me of the day the SS had burned a heap of dead bodies while singing folksongs. I felt I was going to be sick.

A jeep full of English soldiers stopped in front of me. One of the soldiers came over to talk to me. His German was fractured, and it took a while to understand what he was saying.

"Come," he said, "we'll take you a to a refugee shelter."

I wanted to explain that I was not looking for a shelter but for proof that the Nazis had gone. But there was the language problem, and besides, I was too tired to bother. We rode over acres of rubble and then arrived at a relatively unscathed section of town. I looked at the soldiers; so neat and well groomed. The English had been the ones who had driven into the last camp with their tanks. They had surprised the watchtower guards and prevented them from mowing us down with their machine guns as they had promised. The commandant and his crew had fled and left the camp unguarded.

We stopped in front of a villa. Two soldiers took me inside. The hall was crowded with people, sleeping on the floor, huddled in groups, waiting. We pushed our way up the steps and entered a room. Two men rose from behind boxes and files. The soldiers pointed to me. They exchanged information in English. The men nodded. The soldiers saluted and left.

"Sit down," said one of the men in perfect German. "There isn't much we can do, but you can stay here with the others and wait. Do you have any papers?"

I shook my head.

"Have you been deloused?"

I nodded.

The man who spoke wore army trousers and a civilian shirt. He stretched out his hand to help pull me up. The sleeves of my hospital gown rolled back. The man let go of my hand.

"Hans!" he cried, "Look!"

He pointed to the tattoo on my left arm. I was so used to it I barely noticed it.

"Auschwitz," cried the man. "Oh my god! Are you Jewish?"

My heart was racing. It's now or never, I thought, and I said loud and clearly: "Yes, I am."

There was silence. Next, both men kneeled beside me and kissed my hands. They introduced themselves as Hans and Werner Behrenson. Both of them had been in England during the war and had returned to Hamburg to help displaced persons. They insisted I stay. I mentioned the hospital. They assured me they would take care of everything. They turned their bedroom over to me.

"You must have privacy," they said. "Don't be bothered by the others; they are displaced persons—Estonians, Lithuanians, and Croatians, waiting to go home."

They stood by the door, looking awkward.

"We don't know where our parents are. They went on a transport three years ago. Our mother was Jewish, and Father volunteered to go with her. Behrenson. Does that mean anything to you?"

I shook my head.

"Rest well."

They closed the door.

The next day, they came in with a young woman. She was small, with large brown eyes, dressed in a blue skirt and white chiffon blouse. Her name was Erika Stade.

"I've come to rescue you from these men," she said.

She had a lovely smile.

"Hans and Werner are friends of mine," she said. "They told me about you. Please come and stay with me."

"Who is she?" I wondered.

As if reading my mind she said: "I am Jewish myself." She looked at one of the men as if to verify that statement.

"It's true," he said. "You'll be better off at Erika's. You'll get more rest and better company. Besides, it's only two blocks from here."

Erika had a small apartment in a private house. The furniture reminded me of our salon in Osterburg, which Ruth had chosen after much pleading with Father. The furniture was modern and not very comfortable. It hadn't mattered because we never used the salon. "It's Bauhaus style," Erica explained after she saw me touch the furniture. She seemed proud of that style. Next, Erika told me about her affair with a British major, a married man with two children. He was a Colonel Blimp type, jovial and red-cheeked. Erika admitted that his boisterous ways got on her nerves. However, he never stayed long, was amusing, and, of course, he was a good provider. But there had been another affair that bothered Erika's conscience.

"Helmut saved my life. He was a big-shot Nazi, a prominent doctor. He was genuinely in love with me. He got me false papers, took this apartment, and made sure that I was left undisturbed."

She also had an ex-husband with whom she was on good terms. He lived in a small apartment across the street.

"And Helmut," I asked, "Where is he now?"

Erika shrugged her shoulders. "He disappeared shortly before the end. I don't know whether he's dead or alive, and I don't ever want to find out."

Going to bed in Erika's living room, I couldn't fall asleep. Here was this woman who had three men at her feet. She wasn't particularly good looking. In fact, compared to Mrs. Jarz, Erika lacked sex appeal. What was her secret? In camp we were given medication to stop our period. Mine hadn't come back yet. What if I had been rendered sterile?

I looked in the mirror: hollow cheeks, hollow eyes. At least I had my hair. I must have been among the first women who arrived in Auschwitz and didn't have her hair shorn. Now it had grown some more.

Erika offered me some of her clothes. Of course, they had to be altered. Erika knew a seamstress who lived in the country. Mrs. Peterson came one afternoon. She was a woman in her early forties; short and stocky, with cropped gray hair. Looking at me she cried: "My chicken weigh more than you do!"

She invited me to come and live with her for a while. Her family owned a small farm nearby; there would be food and rest. She promised to take good care of me and see to it that I put some weight on.

"Good idea," said the Major. "Come back with a big fanny and some tits and the fellows in my outfit will fall all over you."

I thought it would be a nice change to be out of Erika's house for a while, and I left with Mrs. Peterson. There were no buses or trains, and we had to walk a considerable distance in order to find a running tramway. Luckily, a farmer picked us up with his mule and buggy and drove us to the outskirts of the city from where we had to walk.

It was the beginning of August. The fields were unattended, overgrown with wheat, cornflowers, and poppies. I was exhausted and had to rest. We lay down in the field.

"Our son is missing in action," said Mrs. Peterson. "I want you to understand: we are German but we are decent folk. We didn't know."

At the farm I met her husband, a small, shrunken man who looked old enough to be her father. There also was a grandmother, toothless and hard-of-hearing. The courtyard was overrun with chicken, pigs, and a goat. There was a vegetable garden, a strawberry field, currant bushes, cherry and peach trees. The building was a fieldstone house with stone floors and stone walls, which kept the inside dark and cool. The kitchen had a hearth and an oven made of brick. Instead of running water, there was a pump right next to the sink. The cupboards were filled with crocks, bottles, and jars, containing homemade jams, vinegar, and relishes. Two cats lived on top of the hearth.

My room was on the second floor. It was a tiny chamber, unadorned except for a crucifix and a photo of a bunch of school children. Mrs. Peterson pointed to a grinning boy whose ears stood almost parallel to his face.

"That's my Horst," she said, "He was barely eighteen when he left."

The room contained a massive bed in solid mahogany with hand-carved details. The bed was very high, and I had to hoist myself up into it. Although it was summer, it still had a down featherbed over the mattress, a heavy comforter, and three oversized pillows. The bed faced the window. If I left the outer shutter ajar, in the morning, I could feel the sun on my face and watch the swallows. I waited for the sound of the rooster and then the chiming of the church bells. Next. I could hear the stirring of the household; Mrs. Peterson feeding the chicken. I toyed around with the idea of snatching food from the pantry, setting up my own domain, and never leaving bed.

The grandmother seldom spoke. I helped her clean string beans, hull peas, peel potatoes and carrots. We sat outside in the yard on chairs brought from the kitchen. The yard smelled of hay and cow dung.

Mr. Peterson did not understand who I was, but he accepted me. Mrs. Peterson was half-Dutch and had grown up in Indonesia, a country she spoke of with great affection. She made a dress for me out of a bedspread and was proud of the way I looked now, nicely filled out.

One morning a neighbor came with news: "The Americans dropped an atomic bomb over Japan. The war is over." I was amazed that the Americans had still been fighting. I had assumed the war had been over for everybody.

For the first time, I thought of Lieselotte and Ruth, their husbands Fred and Herman in America. And Father? I could not remember his face.

"What about your family?" Mrs. Peterson had asked early at my stay.

"I have none," I had replied.

In a way that was true. Chances were Father was dead—denounced and deported like me. Or killed by a bomb and buried under heaps of rubble in Berlin, together with Mr. and Mrs. Kraus. And Mrs. Jarz, how could she have survived? It was best not to think. I stayed on, watching the peaches ripen and the brook dry up in the heat. I was getting restless. The days were getting shorter; I felt well and strong. It was time to move on.

Mrs. Peterson understood. "You need to be with other people," she said. "But you have to be careful." She grew pensive. "Erika is nice, but her life is so topsy-turvy; it's not for you."

She suggested I live with an acquaintance of hers. "Mrs. Heilbutt is a very kind person. She too has suffered a lot. She will be good for you."

We walked to the station, again through the fields. This time, I did not have to stop to rest. Also, commuter serviced had been restored. While waiting for the train, Mrs. Person took something out of her pocket and placed it into my hand. It was a gold watch with a heavy chain. My heart was beating. I tried to return the watch. It fell to the floor.

I could see the pile of gold at the receiving station at Auschwitz— watches, wedding rings, amulets, gold teeth—ripped off newly arrived victims before they even dismounted from the train.

Mrs. Peterson picked up the watch.

"I did not mean to offend you," she said. "Forgive me."

I felt sorry. "Never mind," I said.

I pressed her hand into mine.

"Thanks for everything. I will not forget you."

#####

Mrs. Heilbutt lived in Blankenese, once a fashionable suburb of Hamburg. She occupied the top floor of her villa, which was overflowing with tenants who had been there during the war. She begged me to stay.

"I am ashamed to say it, but your moving in would help me evict some of these tenants."

"How is that?"

She explained that the party had confiscated her house because they needed it for families who had been bombed out. They had the right to stay on because there was no place to go.

I was confused. "You are German, aren't you?"

"I am," she said "But my husband was killed by the Nazis, and Peter was in Dachau." It was as if she was apologizing.

"Who is Peter?"

"My son."

"They let me stay in the attic," she continued. "But with the war over and Peter returned, we got the upstairs back to ourselves."

I moved in. My room was oval-shaped with high ceilings and French windows overlooking the garden. The room showed wear and tear: the parquet floor was stained; the glass panels in the door had been replaced by cardboard; the ceiling was discolored from a leak above.

Waking up the next morning, I couldn't remember where I was. From the open window, I saw a huge pine tree that almost blocked the sunlight. A squirrel was hovering between the branches. Its fur was reddish brown. I rose quietly and tiptoed to the window. The squirrel sat on its hind legs, posing with its front paws; its shinny eyes were moving.

"Squirrel," I said, "be my friend," and started to cry.

At that moment I heard a piano playing. I bolted up. Was I hearing right? Someone was playing Beethoven. I went upstairs and entered the room where the playing came from. A young man sat at a baby grand.

"Waldstein?" I asked.

The young man stopped. He looked puzzled. Then he said, "No, Peter Heilbutt."

He bowed slightly. He was tall, lean, with dark curly hair, high forehead, and bushy eyebrows. Unshaven.

"Sorry," he said, "my room is right above yours. I hope my playing doesn't bother you."

I shook my head. "On the contrary," I cried. "Music means everything to me."

"Do you play?"

"I used to. I had this dream of becoming a pianist, imagine."

"What's wrong with that? You're welcome to come up and practice anytime."

After that we grew silent.

"I heard you were in a concentration camp," I said.

He stiffened for a moment, but then he relaxed.

"Dachau."

"How come?"

"Bad luck. I was at my father's office when the Gestapo came to arrest him. He was editor of a left-wing newspaper. He shot himself, so they took me instead."

Peter shrugged his shoulders.

"I never even liked Father. He didn't care about us; he was only interested in politics."

"What about you? Do you have family?"

"I don't know," I said. "I hope so."

I told Peter about Father, Aunt Lizzy, and Uncle Karl.

"You could try to send messages," said Peter. "There is an entire wall here at the old City Hall stuck with notes of people looking for people. They probably do the same thing in Berlin."

I consulted Erika's major.

"It's a hell of a challenge," he said. "Berlin is in the Soviet military zone, which is separated from the English zone by the American one. Berlin itself is subdivided into four zones, so that's like an island, inside the Soviet zone. There's no official communication between either zones. However, occasionally there are orders that take soldiers across the borders. With luck one of your notes could reach Berlin."

He winked at me: "Try it. You have nothing to lose."

I wrote notes, addressing them to Moritz Less, Berlin, stating that I was alive and well and giving my Blankenese address. I took the notes to various army depots and gave them to soldiers, begging them to pass them along so that they would end up in Berlin and to post them at various stations or trees. I also took some notes to Hans and Werner Behrenson, who promised to put them into the right hands.

#####

Like everybody else, the Heilbutts had no food. I was amazed at the injustice. Mrs. Heilbutt waved it aside. "We are Germans like everybody else. The fact that Peter was a political prisoner in Dachau doesn't count. There are a lot of deserters claiming they were camp prisoners, including the SS men. The authorities are trying to sort things out." She patted Peter's hand.

"As long as I have my Peter back, it doesn't matter."

Getting food was no problem for me. I fact, there was little I could not obtain. I had received identity papers with AUSCHWITZ written on them. The word worked miracles; it entitled me to privileges beyond anything I needed. I went to the English dispensary and received money; I received invitations to live with families and was offered study grants from Sweden and Switzerland.

Most of the supplies were CARE packages from America. They contained tins and boxes with strange items. I brought everything to Blankenese. Since none of us could read the labels, we sat around the kitchen table and tried to guess what all the items were. Strangest of all was a box which contained dry flakes. The three of us tried to decide if they should be cooked or eaten raw. The coffee, however, was good. Mrs. Heilbutt brewed some in the morning and neighbors came just to get a whiff of the aroma.

One morning Peter mentioned that members of the former Hamburg Staatsopera were going to perform Brahms's "German Requiem."

"Would you like to come?" he asked.

The Requiem, I thought. Oh no.

"It's Brahms' most profound work," Peter continued. "Do you know it?"

Did I know it?

Denn alles Fleisch es ist wie Gras
und alle Herrlichkeit des Menschen wie des Grases Blumen.

(For all flesh is as grass,
and all the glory of man as the flower of grass)

I sang those words in my head while burying the dead bodies. I had volunteered for the job since it enabled me to get out of the freight car where we were packed like so much garbage. We had left the Hempstead camp to flee from the advancing Russian army and were now in search of another camp. We received no food or water. People screamed; some went crazy. There was no toilet facility. The car stank beyond belief. The SS sealed the car and only opened it in the mornings when they came to throw out the dead. They used the ends of their rifles for inspection; whoever did not move was pushed out. Some had their eyes open, others closed. I'd grab an arm, or a leg, and help carry the load. It took four of us to bury one. We tossed them into quickly dug pits and turned to fetch the next one.

I was barely aware of what I was doing. Day in day out, it was the same routine. We were on a merry-go-round, with the wheels clicking over the same rails. All those bodies! We dumped them often in the old burial grounds, encircled by vultures.

Das Gras ist verdorret und die Blume abgefallen.
(The grass withers, and the flower falleth away.)

I looked at Peter. "I'm sick and tired of German composers," I said defiantly.

Peter stared at me in disbelief. I took him a minute to regain his composure. "Well," he said, "there's always Chopin, Dvorak, Smetana, Grieg; not to forget the three M's: Mendelssohn, Mussorgsky, and Massenet."

"Ah, the degenerate ones. " I had to smile. "I didn't mean to bad-mouth Brahms, it's just that I have a bad association with his Requiem."

Peter put one arm around my shoulder and nodded: "I understand."

Close to the English depot was the black market. That's where I met Johnny, obviously a big shot because he rode a motorcycle. It was hard to guess his age. He had thinning red hair and skin like parchment, colorless except for his freckles. His past was questionable. He had worked for the resistance by helping them smuggle people into Denmark; at the same time he had been buying and selling stolen art work for the Nazis. Now he was active on the black market and well connected both with the underworld and with the military high command.

"Don't be so damned sensitive about your Auschwitz number," he said. "Here." He showed me his tattoo—a voluptuous mermaid on his upper left arm. I became his protégé.

"You and I are alike," he boasted. "Tough as nails. We could take over the country. Remember Hitler—tomorrow the world? What an asshole."

Johnny introduced me to one of his clients, Thomas, whose full name was Baron Ludwig Friederich Thomas von Bülow. His handkerchiefs and ascots bore the family coat of arms; his face was marred by the dueling scar which he had received while a student in Heidelberg. Years ago, his father had killed himself over a minor incident with the party. It had left Thomas's family above political suspicion and permitted certain privileges. Thomas found that amusing. I couldn't understand why he bothered about me. I made fun of his pretensions, yet he courted me. He sent me flowers and hand-bound volumes of poetry. I liked his attentions, particularly since—aside from a bad limp that had helped him stay out of the army—he was good looking.

Thomas lived on the family estate on the outskirts of Hamburg. There had been considerable destruction: The stables, barns, carriage houses, and two entire wings had all been demolished. The manor house, however, was in livable condition. The most comfortable room was the library, the domain of Thomas's mother. She was an invalid who spent her days sitting in a specially constructed chair, her legs covered by a plaid blanket. Her mind wandered, and she said silly things. Thomas never discussed her illness. Thomas was an excellent chess player, and we spent hours involved in intense games while he played music from the family's record collection, which contained entire Verdi operas, all of Beethoven's symphonies, and vintage recordings of Chaliapin and Kipnis. If I stayed for lunch, we would take it in the dining room, surrounded by family portraits and hunting trophies. The meal would be a dish of kale or turnips served by the only remaining servant.

I settled into a routine. I practiced piano for two to three hours at Mrs. Heilbutt's baby grand and studied with a teacher recommended by Peter. Two or three times a week I went to Hamburg. Because of the early curfew, I either stayed at Erika's or at her ex-husband's apartment.

Returning to Blankenese one day, I saw the letters on the desk. They were from Father and Mrs. Jarz. I studied the envelopes. It was a mystery how they had reached me. I didn't dare open them out of fear the news might not be all that good. I took the letters and went into the garden. It was the end of October; winter was in the air. The ground was like a soft carpet, covered with layers of fallen leaves. In the distance I could hear the foghorn of the Ulster ferry. I leaned against a tree and closed my eyes. My hand was shaking, and I dropped the letters. I picked up the letters; my lips were quivering. I opened Mrs. Jarz's letter and started to read. The letter was overflowing with expressions of love and tender feelings, her impatience for us to be reunited, and her own happiness at being together with Father again in a small apartment in the American zone. I studied her handwriting. I loved the way she rounded her *e*'s and *a*'s. Father's writing was more distinctive—a combination of old-fashioned Gothic script and precise printing.

"My darling precious daughter," I read, "my prayers have been answered. You are alive, and I consider myself blessed beyond belief to have you safely returned to me."

He went on to say that Tante Lizzy and Uncle Karl were fine and thrilled to hear that I was well. I put my arms around the tree and rubbed my face against the bark till it hurt. I remembered outings with Father when I was about five years old. The smell of moss and fern had been similar, but it had mingled with the scent of chocolate that Father had hidden for me to find.

"I could die now," I thought. "I will never be as happy again."

For the next few days, I was elated. I told everybody the news and reveled in their good wishes. Then my mood changed. The more I thought about returning to Berlin the less I liked it. The bargain had been fulfilled: I was alive and Father was alive. It had been so painful having to learn to do without my family. Why start all over again? I cherished my life in Hamburg, my independence, my privileged status, and my new friends.

Peter for one.

"I'll stay if you want me to," I said.

He shook his head.

"I don't know what I am going to do myself. If it weren't for Mother I would have left Hamburg already. I can't stand it; it's so corrupt."

I decided to pay a surprise visit to Thomas. I found him in the study of his estate, dressed in riding habit cleaning his pistol.

"Think of committing suicide?" I asked.

He shoved the weapon toward me.

"Do you know how to use it?"

Actually I didn't, but I had been tempted to use it once.

There had been that scene in Auschwitz. It must have been at least a month after I arrived that one of the inmates had tried to escape, and we had been ordered to watch her execution. The girl was tied to a pole, stripped naked. As usual, during assembly, I stood in the front row. I had realized that those of us brazen enough to be in full view were the least likely to be harassed by the guards. An SS man stopped in front of the girl next to me. He drew a revolver out of his holster and pressed it into her hand.

"You shoot her," he commanded. "Go ahead. Let me see you pull the trigger."

The girl dropped the gun. The SS man hit her so hard, she fell to the floor. Next he moved on to me. I raised my head and looked him straight into the eyes. He picked up the weapon and twirled it in his hand.

"If he orders me to shoot, I'll kill him," I vowed.

I emptied my head of any thought so as not to betray myself. I held my gaze steady and did not blink. I noticed a faint smile on his face, and he moved on.

I looked at Thomas and wondered why I had bothered with him. He was a mama's boy, a spoiled brat.

"Go to hell," I said and left.

I had to see Johnny. At least he didn't pretend. Luckily I found him home.

"Take me to the Reperbahn," I said.

"Are you crazy?"

"I want to go to Sao Paoli."

Johnny shook his head. "What's the matter with you? You know very well that place is only for pimps and hookers. So cut it out."

"You cut it out," I yelled. "What's so special about me that I can't be with whores?"

"Please," said Johnny, "I am tired, and it's late. We'll go some other time."

"No," I yelled, "I want to go now!"

Johnny shook his head. "I don't know what's gotten into you. Jesus Christ, woman. Wait, I'll get dressed."

While Hamburg was shut down by the curfew and was dark and gloomy, the Reperbahn, Hamburg's red-light district, was ablaze with neon lights.

"Supposedly they keep it open for the occupation," said Johnny. "Baloney. It's full of war criminals hiding out, in addition to the usual riff raff. In case we get separated, remember, it's every man for himself."

I wanted to remind him that where I had been, women and children hadn't exactly come first, but I got distracted by the sights of the hookers. They sat in small windows, displaying their bosoms and thighs, frizzy hair, false eye-lashes, and beauty marks. They wore velvet ribbons, garter belts, and lace. I remembered them stinking out of every pore of their open sores, rotting away with syphilis. They all had died sooner or later. Sometimes, having to share a bunk with one of them, I had simply kicked her out.

We entered a bar so filled with smoke I almost missed the two women wrestling in the mud. Johnny ordered beer, which he urged me to chase down with an icy liquid.

"Aquavit," he said. "It will put hair on your chest."

He was busy with two girls sitting in his lap. The three were giggling. There was a telephone on the table which rang constantly. I wanted to answer it, but had trouble reaching the receiver. A fat guy came over and started to get familiar. I tried to push him away, which he thought amusing. Johnny waved his arms.

"She's with me."

The guy belched and put his arms around me. Johnny grabbed him by his belt, but all this accomplished was to pull down his trousers down to his knees. The guy let go of me to slug Johnny but missed. I felt sick and realized that by the time the man was ready to paw me again, I was going to throw up. At that moment I heard sirens. The lights went out; everybody was screaming, scrambling towards the door. For a moment I thought it was an air raid, but then I remembered the war was over. Within minutes the MPs had everybody lined up. They were checking papers and hauled everybody into police vans. When I showed them my identity card, they saluted and told me to stand aside.

"Johnny," I pointed him out. He's with me."

They nodded and let him slip out. Two MPs were assigned to drive me home. There was a full moon, and I recognized the Milky Way.

"Twinkle, twinkle little star," went through my head. I felt two years old. The soldiers waited till I was safely inside. I entered my room and sat on the bed, holding my splitting head.

It was time to go home.

Two days later, I left. I had bought a brand new white fur jacket on the black market. Although hardly suitable for the journey, I thought it was proper attire for my entry into Berlin. I took provision for three days, as well as chocolate, cigarettes, a bottle of Schnapps, nylon stockings, salami, and other items that might come in handy.

My Return to Berlin
December 1945

Railroad depots and trains; the morning mist of the freight yard; the noisy assembling of cars into trains; lanterns appearing out of nowhere; the clanging, banging and whistling. How familiar.

It was dark, damp, and bitter cold. There was a slight rain mixed with snow flurries. My fur jacket smelled of goat.

"This is crazy," I thought. "I should go back and wait for a better season."

I almost failed before I started. Twice the English chased me off the premises; trains were either guarded or sealed. Finally, I convinced an old workman to break one of the locks and to smuggle me into a car that was heading east.

I took a nap.

I wondered what had happened to Fritzi. I had stayed in Auschwitz for about five months but didn't meet Fritzi until we were both on the train that took inmates out because of the advancing Russians. Fritzi said she had been in camp for two years; she was amazingly plump. I wondered how that was possible.

"Protection," she said, "I got protection from the camp doctor."

"The camp doctor? That was a woman!"

"So?"

I blushed.

Fritzi took no notice. She chatted on about her wardrobe: closets brimming with furs, velvet suits, satin, taffeta, skirts slit up to the knee, riding outfits, feathers, bows, hats.

We stopped frequently while wagons were being unhitched and the train reassembled till we were the only car left. It was cold; I shivered in my tattered dress. We stopped. The station read "Helmstedt." SS men appeared and ordered us out. We trotted through the deep snow, a tired bunch of bedraggled prisoners, thirty in all.

The camp was small. There were the usual barbed wire, armed patrol on the watch towers, a courtyard, and two barracks. The camp commandant was a young woman. She sat at the head of the table, flanked by two assistants. She was statuesque. Her blond hair was done up in a chignon.

Fritzi and I were first in line for the admission procedure. Fritzi sniffed. "Frau Commandant," she said, "you are wearing my favorite cologne, Maria Farina." The woman frowned. Fritzi pressed on.

"I see you have style. It's rare these days. I am a couturier and could make some dresses for you."

"You are fresh," said the woman. "But your style isn't bad either." She paused. "What else can you do?"

Without a word, Fritzi placed a foot on the chair. Hands on hips, she leaned forward seductively as she sang: "Ich bin von Kopf bis Fuss auf Liebe eingestelt ..." (I am designed for love from head to toe...) She was no Marlene Dietrich, but she was something.

The commandant laughed. "You are some number. Where are you from?"

"Vienna."

"We could do with some fun here."

"I am available," said Fritzi. "What would you like me to do?"

The women consulted with each other. "First thing, we will put you in charge of the Jews. Second, your quarters will be next to ours. Then we will see."

Fritzi curtsied slightly. "I kiss your hand, Frau Kommandant. I promise I'll be worthy of the honor."

"You better. We are inmates ourselves. The SS live in the villa

*across the street. We have a free hand here, but we keep strict discipline.
It's our head, you understand. Get your people moving."*

*My heart beat wildly. This was my chance. I should put my arm
around Fritzi and say: "Me too. Protect me." Maybe I should sing
the drinking song from "Die Feldermaus" (The Bat): "S' its mal bei
uns so Sitte, chacun a son gout." (It's simply my custom ...) I'd be a
hit. Yet I did not move. What was the matter with me? I was a dumb
kid—a provincial and a coward.*

*In line with the others, I received my uniform. A coarse garment
with blue and gray stripes and the yellow triangle. I did not lift my
head for fear I would meet Fritzi's gaze. But I heard her voice. She
had taken charge: "Move, move! We don't have all day."*

*Everything was stone and mortar. It smelled of chlorine and
green soap. We entered one big room and made ourselves comfortable
as best we could in a long row of bunk beds.*

*It was still dark at roll call. We lined up on one side of the corridor,
facing the group of other inmates. They were social offenders—
prostitutes and criminals.*

*It was the first time we shared quarters with German inmates.
They hated us.*

*"Dirty Jews," they shouted. "Get out of our camp!" Some spat
across the hall.*

The commandant arrived, followed by her companions and Fritzi.

*"She'll single me out now," I thought. She'll point to me and say
I'm too nice for all of this."*

But Fritzi walked straight past, busy counting.

*The commandant addressed us: "You have been shipped here to
work in the salt mines. If you don't work your quota, or miss roll call,
you'll be punished."*

*Led by a small patrol, we walked out of camp through a small,
shabby village. It was bitter cold. The few people we encountered
turned their backs. The mine elevator took twenty people at a time.
We rode down in total darkness.*

*The first chamber was gray; as we walked along they became
white. Left and right there were big caves, glittering as if studded*

with diamonds. The path was lit by meager bulbs. There was a strong smell of iodine. It was very quiet.

Suddenly there were blazing lights and deafening noise. A huge hall revealed rows of heavy machinery, lorries, bins, and workers.

I was dumbfounded. A munitions factory. The workers—all women—hardly bothered to look up as we passed. They assigned each of us to a machine.

The routine was roll call at dawn; into the mines, work; walk back; another roll call. By that time it was dark. Often I was too tired to eat.

My wrists and ankles were swollen and they ached. Everyone had similar complaints. "It's the salt; it makes your body retain fluid. It's the food. They put chemical stuff into it. "

I was nauseous all the time. I suffered from dizzy spells. The long walk to and from work exhausted me. I had to rest, if only for a few days. I went to the infirmary.

The attendant said: "No Jews here."

Fritzi caught sight of me in the hall. She barely recognized me: "Is that you? You look terrible."

"I need to rest. I'm sick."

Fritzi was taken aback.

"Wait, I'll be right back."

She returned a few minutes later.

"It's all arranged. Come."

She turned me over to the infirmary attendant, talking to her in a hushed voice. She took my hand.

"Rest for a few days, and don't be angry with me."

"I'm not. Thank you." I smiled. "I kiss your hand, Fritzi."

By evening, we entered the American zone where I had to change trains. I spent the night in a broken-down tool shed. At daybreak, I saw a train marked DRESDEN. Knowing that Dresden was in the Eastern Zone, I climbed into a car, hoping for the best. The crucial moment would come at the Russian checkpoint. It was there that they raped any woman foolish enough to appear. I could scream "Auschwitz" till I was blue in my face; they would not pause long enough to listen.

I went to see the engineer in charge of the locomotive. He was an elderly man, covered with soot. I showed him the cigarettes and hinted at the schnapps.

"Imagine I'm your daughter," I said. "You would protect me, surely. I bet you know a way to outsmart them."

He liked that. He hid me in the coal bin—a small box, half filled with coal. He closed the lid and left me to wheeze and sneeze. It happened fast. I heard screaming and shooting. We must be at the border. What if the engineer forgot about me? I would suffocate. "Oh my God," I thought, "I must not panic."

I had to divert my thoughts. Stage some music; a light and frothy song to celebrate my return to Berlin "Das ist Berlin, Berlin die schönste Stadt der Welt" (That is Berlin, Berlin, the most beautiful city of the world) went through my head.

I had given my best concert at Auschwitz. It occurred on the first evening of our arrival at camp. After a two-day journey, we had stumbled onto the train platform, joined by people from other cars. We were stripped naked and stood in the blazing sun while men in prison uniforms searched our bodies for gold. An SS man appeared. He removed one glove and casually pointed at the tailor, Dr. Irene, the little girls and several other people—"left," he said. Katjia, Dr. Magnus, and I stepped "right," as directed. When they separated men and women, all hell broke lose. People were screaming and wailing. Some fell on their knees and implored the SS man to let them go with their loved ones. The SS man beat them with his whip. Our little group was ushered into a washroom where women in prison uniforms tattooed numbers on our arms and cropped our hair short.

"You are the first arrival not to get shorn," they informed us. They wondered why. Next, we were led into an adjacent room where showerheads above pelted us with ice cold water. We each received a prison uniform marked with a yellow triangle and marched through a barbed-wire gate with a sign: "Eine Laus Dein Todt." (One Louse Your Death)

The sun was setting; it was getting chilly. As directed, we assembled in front of our assigned barrack with the other inmates. All the inmates of the A camp stood in front of their barracks. There must have been hundreds. It was getting dark and still we stood. I noticed black smoke curling toward the red horizon.

"What is that?" I whispered to the girl next to me.

"Ssh, don't talk."

A few minutes later, she whispered: "The ovens. They are burning the elderly and the children."

"They are burning the children?" My question hung in the air, changing everything around me. People, barracks, sky disappeared. "It's not true," I thought. "This cannot be. I cannot live with it. I'll go crazy."

That's when the concert came into my head. Nothing but a piano concerto would do. I pictured myself dressed all in white; my blond hair was cascading down to my shoulders. I walked onto the stage, passed the members of the orchestra. The audience greeted me with a warm applause. I bowed and smiled. The piano was an eight-foot Bechstein; the best of the best. I adjusted the piano bench and sat down. The conductor raised his baton and gave the downbeat to the orchestra. The string players first, joined by the woodwind and brass. I placed my hands on the keyboard. The conductor nodded. I started playing. The sweet sound of Mozart's A Major Concerto filled the air.

Trapped in the coal box, I felt the train come to a sudden halt. As promised, the engineer came to collect me. My legs gave way, and I fell to the ground. He laughed.

"You look like a chimneysweep. Not even the Russians would touch you now."

Some joke. My fur jacket was ruined; I had to leave it behind. I gave the engineer the schnapps, plus a can of sardines. He was touched. He asked around about trains going toward Berlin and escorted me to the right one.

"Good luck." He tipped his cap.

I settled in the caboose, which had a bench and open windows all around. I was cold without a coat. But I felt good and treated myself to the remainder of the salami, spitting the skin out of the window. The trains had a nice rhythm.

We slowed down. Suddenly the door opened, and two men stumbled in. I was too startled to notice that they were Russian soldiers. I could feel their holsters pressing again my ribs. They smelled of liquor and sweat. My heart beat. Good God! Would they rape me, standing up, on a moving train? What to do? I could kill them; throw them off the train. Instead I started to hum the "Third International." The guys joined in. They had lusty baritone voices. We sang the anthem three times before we switched to "Otchi-Tchornia."

The fellow on my right rolled up his sleeves and displayed a row of wristwatches up to his elbow.

"Uri, uri," he said proudly.

I patted him. "Great."

He removed one watch and put in on my arm.

"*Tovarichie.*"

They offered me vodka. It burned my insides, but made me nice and warm. I kept my eyes on the scenery. I recognized the station—SPANDAU. We were close. When the train slowed down, I jumped out.

The Russians leaned out.

"*Do-Svidania.*"

I waved. They looked like two grinning schoolboys.

I walked toward the station and found a commuter train in service. Like Hamburg, Berlin, too, was a heap of rubble.

CHARLOTTENBURG. This is where the royal palace was. On our first visit to Berlin, Father had taken me on a sightseeing tour. I listened to his proud account of the Hohenzoller dynasty and had felt part of it.

WESTKREUZ. I became agitated. How would it be? Would I have to listen to Father again? I had grown up.

SAVINGPLATZ

ZOOLIGISCHER GARDTEN

My stop. I relaxed. Suddenly I felt impatient to get home. I got off the train.

"Ticket, please."

The platform attendant touched my elbow.

"What ticket?"

"Mensch, don't act dumb. You are holding up traffic."

I thought it amusing. "If you must know, I come all the way from Hamburg. How much is that?"

He looked puzzled for a moment. But then he said sternly: "There's no service from Hamburg."

"Damn right. Now let me pass."

His yes opened wide. "Pass? Not so fast, Miss. There still is law and order in Germany. I'll teach you a lesson."

"I'll teach you a lesson!" I yelled. I pushed up my sleeve, exposing my Auschwitz number.

"Here," I screamed. "Here is my ticket. I paid."

A crowd had gathered. An American MP appeared.

"What's going on here?"

"You haven't won the war," I shouted. "Nothing has changed. You dropped your bomb on the wrong people!"

He touched my shoulder.

"Take it easy, Miss."

The spire of the Kaiser Wilhelm Gedächniskirche was broken off; the church was a burned-out hull. Once this had been the swankiest neighborhood in Berlin. In her letter Mrs. Jarz had written that they had been given a pleasant ground-floor apartment in a street facing the zoo. There were no animals. Presumably they were still in exile.

"An elephant consumes an average of two hundred pounds of grain a day," Father had told me.

Now here was some useful information. Something I could believe in.

A man stood in front of a house, gathering firewood from a neatly assembled pile. His heavy-knit cardigan hung loosely around his thin frame. Some wood slipped out of his arm. He bent to retrieve it. His left hand was crippled.

Epilogue

Father and I were on the boat train to Bremerhaven. From there, we would sail on the first troop ship to take refugees to America. Lieselotte and Ruth had arranged for our visas and passage.

Berlin had reeked of defeat: a dead city cloaked in stunned silence. Father and Mrs. Jarz lived in a three-room apartment. The place had no gas or electricity; water was frozen in the pipes. There was a daily ration of potatoes—nothing else. Father bought the rest on the black market.

Father was in good spirits, but Mrs. Jarz said she could not sleep. She had returned from Theresienstadt with a kidney disease. Aunt Lizzy and Uncle Karl looked upon my return as an act of God. They lived in the old apartment with the windows guttered up, cracked walls, and no plumbing. Father had stayed with them until the end, when he became a hero. Karlshorst was the scene of one of the last skirmishes between the Germans and the Russians. Anxious to prevent further bloodshed, Father had run into the street, waving a big white handkerchief. With his childhood Russian, he confronted the looting soldiers and by sheer force of authority, prevented them from raping the women. The Russians wanted to make him deputy mayor, but Father declined.

The compartment was empty. We took the window seats.

The first time Father and I had traveled on a train was to attend Mutti's funeral in Berlin. I hoped Father wouldn't cry again as he had when he received the phone call that Mutti had died. She had been in the hospital; everything was fine and she was expected to come home in a few days. But something unforeseen must have happened because instead she had died. To prevent Father from crying, I tried to entertain him.

"I know the multiplication table," I said proudly. "Would you like to hear?"

Father shook his head. "Some other time."

I was saved from further efforts by a man who entered our compartment. He said he was a traveling salesman. He pointed to me. "What a sweet little girl. She must be the apple of your eyes."

Father frowned. Then he said: "We are in mourning."

The salesman expressed his condolence. The two talked about illness and hospitals. I looked at the passing scenery.

Father rubbed his hands. "What do you say? We actually made it!"

He looked dapper in a gray suit tailored for our journey. I felt a tremendous surge of affection for him and would have kissed him except I knew Father didn't like emotional displays.

The door to our apartment opened.

"May I?" A young man entered. He was handsome, with strong features, a sensuous mouth, and dark hair.

"By all means," said Father.

"Viktor Steinhardt," the man introduced himself.

Father extended his hand.

"Pleased to meet you. We are on our way to America."

"So am I."

"Meet my daughter."

I blushed. I watched the man arrange his luggage and settle into the corner across from me. His presence seemed to fill the compartment.

"We are moving!" called Father. "We are on our way." He

opened the window. The three of us leaned out and watched the city disappear.

We took our seats. I felt the man studying me. He leaned forward.

"My cousin has a dry cleaning store in Brooklyn," he said. "I am going to learn the business."

He moved closer.

"What are you going to do in America?"

I felt a new sensation. It was a joy that sprang from the very pit of my navel and reached all the way up to may face and made me smile.

"I am going to study music," I said.

Me, Then

Our house and store in Osterburg

With my sisters Ruth and Lieselotte

Father in Berlin

Berlin outing with Father and friend

Mrs. Jarz

Lizzy Kraus

Time Line

1938

November 7	Ernst von Rath, third secretary in the German Embassy in Paris, shot and killed by a Polish Jew.
November 9	*Kristallnacht* (Crystal Night)
November 11	German Jews fined one million marks in aftermath of *Kristallnacht*
November 15	Expulsion of Jewish pupils from German schools
	Decree of compulsory Aryanization of all Jewish enterprises and shops

1939

September 1	German invasion of Poland (Beginning of World War II)

September 1	Jews forbidden to be outdoors after eight P.M. in the winter and nine P.M. in the summer
September 3	Declaration of war on Germany by Great Britain and France
September 23	Jews forbidden to own radios

1940

February 12	First deportation of Jews from Germany

1941

March 7	Employment of Jews for compulsory labor inside Germany
September 1	Jews have to wear a yellow star with the word "Jew" imprinted
October	Mass deportation of German Jews begins
December 7	Pearl Harbor attacked by Japanese
December 11	Hitler declares war on the United States

1942

April 20	Ban on the use of public transportation by Jews
June 23	First gassing at Auschwitz

September 28	Reduction of food rations for Jews
November 7–8	Landing of American and British troops on the coast of North Africa
November 19–22	Russian counteroffensive at Stalingrad

1943

February 2	Stalingrad retaken by Russian troops
February 27	Jews employed in Berlin armaments industry sent to Auschwitz
May 19	Berlin declared *Judenfrei* (free of Jews)
June 10	Allied landing in Sicily
September 8	Announcement of surrender of Italy
November 6	Kiev recaptured by the Russians

1944

June 6, 1944	D-Day Allied troops land in Normandy

1945

January 18	Evacuation of some 66,000

	prisoners from Auschwitz
January 27	The Russians enter Auschwitz
April 30	Hitler commits suicide
May 7	Germany surrenders to Allies; war ends in Europe

About the Author

Helen Studley was born in Germany and, as a Jew, experienced the full impact of Nazi persecution. She came to United States after World War II, became a musicologist, opened a travel agency, and owned a restaurant. She is the author of two cookbooks and is a freelance travel, food, and lifestyle writer. She and her husband, George, live in New York City.